NORMAN SPLENDOUR

Duiske Abbey
Graignamanagh

NORMAN SPLENDOUR

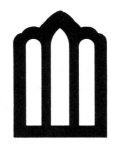

Duiske Abbey
Graignamanagh

Geraldine Carville

Blackstaff Press

Published by Blackstaff Press Limited, 255A Upper
Newtownards Road, Belfast BT4 3JF, Northern
Ireland.

ISBN 0 85640 171 4

Printed in Northern Ireland by Belfast Litho
Printers Limited.

Frontispiece— Aerial photograph of Graignamanagh: Tom Brett

Contents

List of Illustrations

Photos by courtesy of Tom Brett, Kilkenny: Cover, frontispiece, p14, p23, p24, p26, p30, p35, p36, p38, p40, p41, p53, p54, p75, p78, p79, p82, p84, p85, p93, p94, p98, p99, p101, p106.

Foreword

Norman Splendour is a fascinating book. It is centred on Duiske Abbey, Graiguenamanagh, but its reach and its breadth open up for us a new vision of the monastic and social history of mediaeval Ireland.

It was in 1180 that an Irish Chief, Dermot O'Ryan, wished to build a Benedictine Abbey where the streamlet Dubh Uisce flowed into the river Barrow. But the Norman invasion intervened and in 1204 it was a Cistercian Abbey which was founded by the new Norman overlords.

Miss Carville's historical account is the product of meticulous research with unvarying adherence to the highest standards of scholarship. Not merely does she give us the facts of the original foundation, but she has been able to trace the progress of the actual building of the Abbey. She identifies the source of the stone, the slates, the sand. We are told of the masons, stone-cutters and other skilled tradesmen who were brought to the site and whose families settled about a mile east of the Abbey.

Miss Carville draws upon her unrivalled knowledge of Cistercian history to describe the every-day life of the Abbey. She portrays the monks with their virtues and their faults; they quarrelled among themselves; they fought with outsiders; they feuded with the neighbouring Abbey of Jerpoint, but they also worked and prayed. The Abbey became the centre of worship for the people of the surrounding countryside; the town grew under the shadow of its walls; new skills were introduced; improved methods of agriculture were put into operation and a thriving export trade was established.

The history of the sixteenth century suppression of the Abbey is laid before us. The Abbey was sentenced to death, but it stubbornly refused to die. Fugitive monks continued to serve the people, and even when the roof fell in the people of Graiguenamanagh erected a small 'mass-house' near the south transept, and so preserved the precious link of Mass and public worship until they returned to a partially repaired Abbey Church in the last century.

All this and more is contained in *Norman Splendour* — a work of consummate scholarship which is a major contribution to Irish historical studies.

Bishop Patrick Lennon

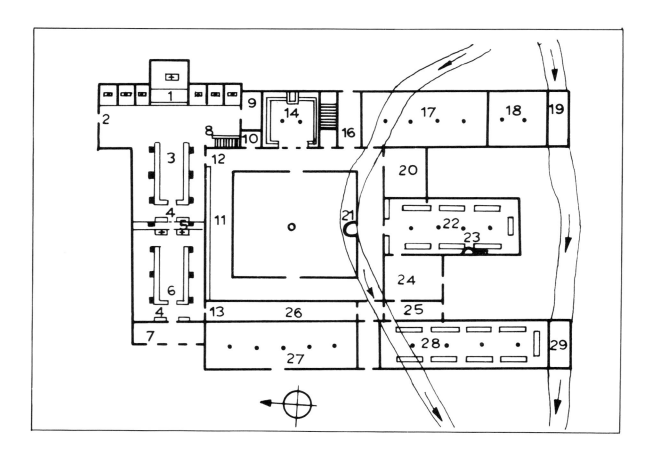

The ideal Cistercian Monastery as presented by Aubert and Dimier.

Introduction

In 1970, I received a letter from Fr Killian, OCSO, Mt Mellerey Abbey, Co Waterford, describing how the parishioners of Graignamanagh were considering the restoration of Graignamanagh Abbey, which in the Medieval period, was one of the largest in Europe. He also enclosed a newspaper cutting 'Abbey in Crisis' which Fr Athanasius had prepared and published. He encouraged me to visit Graignamanagh and the following Easter I visited Duiske Abbey for the first time and I was fascinated and impressed. Here was an Abbey Church approaching a Cathedral in size, in which there has been a continuity of worship since 1220 and where the people in conversation speak of 'Our Abbey'. Generations of parishioners have preserved the Abbey Church itself and many have incorporated its Claustral buildings in their homes. 'Come into my office and you will see the windows of the Scriptorium', 'Come into my garden and you will see the reader's gallery' whilst another will say, 'The great drain passes under my office.' Walk through the Turf Market, past Peg Washington's Lane, and converge on the Abbey Hotel and you are at the former Porter's Gate: the Abbey Complex has governed the morphology of the town. Of the thirty-four Cistercian Abbeys in Medieval Ireland Duiske Abbey has the most extant remains. Duiske Abbey is different, I thought to myself in 1971 but why was the question I had to answer. Gradually as I researched its Historical Geography I realised that much was attributable to its Norman origin and every aspect increased my wonder and admiration and on New Year's Eve 1976, in Mount Mellerey Abbey Co Waterford I revealed to Fr Killian OCSO RIP and Fr Athanasius OCSO that *Norman Splendour: Duiske Abbey* was ready for publication.

In July 1976 I was in Graignamanagh once more and I decided that in addition to the full book a guide should be prepared from it for quick reading and this I have called *'Duiske Abbey; A Town Remembers'*.

I wish to thank many people whom I associate with this book. I thank Fr Killian OCSO RIP and Fr Athanasius who aroused my interest. I thank the Abbot of Mellifont, Dom Enda, the Prior, Fr Lawrence, and Fr Colmcille who came with me on a visit to Duiske Abbey. I thank the Parish Priest of Graignamanagh Fr Gavin, the curate Fr Dunny and the people of Graignamanagh at home and abroad for their enthusiasm which moved me to write this book. To the Hughes family of Sillare, Graignamanagh, my sincere thanks and to Fr Wm. Gavin who read my manuscript and Right Rev Dom Aengus, Bethlehem Abbey, Portglenone, Co Antrim who proofed this book, chapter by chapter, my sincere thanks.

Geraldine Carville

Celtic Sites in Medieval Ireland

The Celtic Twilight

There were thirty-four Cistercian Abbeys in Medieval Ireland, some of which were established on Celtic sites which had been abandoned, or in which there were active communities from which a transfer of personnel to the Cistercian Order took place. As the story of Duiske Abbey unfolds it will be seen that an understanding of the Celtic system is essential to the study of Cistercian Medieval Abbeys, particularly in the dioceses of Leighlin and Ossory, in which were situated the Cistercian Abbeys of Jerpoint, Killenny, Baltinglass, Abbeyleix and Duiske.

Until the fifth century AD Ireland was pagan. Shortly afterwards Pope Celestine sent Paladius to the small colonies of Christians in south east Ireland. In 432 Patrick, later St Patrick, came to Ireland and it was during his lifetime that one of the first monastic settlements took place on the south east coast at Dair Inis, Co Waterford.[1] During the sixth and seventh centuries, Celtic monasticism grew rapidly and took on a missionary aspect. Two outstanding monks of this period were St Finnian of Clonard and St Enda of Aran. The former in particular, by the founding of the great monastic school of Clonard which is said to have numbered its pupils in thousands, came to exercise a great influence over the whole of Ireland and Finnian became popularly known as the teacher of the Saints of Ireland. Twelve of the best known monastic founders were later grouped together by hagiographers under the title of 'Twelve Apostles of Ireland' and were credited with having received their monastic education at the School of Clonard. However, many of the so-called 'Twelve Apostles of Ireland' could not in fact have been pupils of St Finnian of Clonard, since some of them had died long before his time, while others were not born until after his own death. Nevertheless the legend thus recorded bears witness to the great influence exercised by St Finnian in the Ireland of his day.

Each of these early monasteries was independent and exercised control over a great number of scattered daughter houses. None of the Celtic monasteries derived much benefit from the ecclesiastical organisation before 1152 when bishoprics were created. Some monks bore the title of bishop. They had however, no general jurisdiction over the organisation of the monasteries nor any authority over their economic policies. They were concerned primarily with ritual matters such as the ordination of priests, consecration of bishops and the administration of the sacraments. Each monastic Fine had an Abbot who was responsible for the jurisdiction not only of his own Abbey but also of any daughter houses which might have been established. This required so much attention that the Abbot was frequently away on circuit.

Some of the Celtic monasteries supported groups of anchorites from whom the monastic bishops, scribes and masters of the school were often

12

recruited. Also, along with providing scope for religious life, the monasteries fulfilled a number of ancillary functions such as running schools. Some were important pilgrimage centres, others housed penitents over long periods. Then there were the craftsmen whose workshops produced reliquaries and shrines. Hence many of the Celtic monasteries were characterised by a diverse and active population - so much so that some monks found all this activity disturbing to their religious life and decided to leave the bustle of the large monastery,

often known as a Civites, in order to retire to secluded places. Favourite sites were small islands in nearby lakes. The population of these secluded houses so increased that new settlements were founded in other remote places, such as islands in other lakes, or off the coast. In this way a hierarchy of monastic settlements developed. The ultimate size was dependent on three main circumstances: the nodality and accessibility of the monastery, the relative fame of the founder saint's tomb and famous schools attached to monasteries. A dead

The Old Celtic Church site of St Michael, Tinna-hinch.

founder renowned for holiness would draw crowds of pilgrims, a noteworthy centre in this area being St Moling.

The Celtic monastic foundations went from strength to strength until the end of the eighth century. By then the Norse raids had begun. The Norsemen were principally interested in plunder. The average rural settlement had little to offer and the absence of towns meant that the monasteries themselves provided the most likely source of precious metals and other valuables. At first only the coastal sites were attacked, but later the Norsemen penetrated inland to those Abbeys easily approached by river routes. Plunder was sometimes accomplished by deliberate destruction of monastic buildings and slaughter of the monks themselves. The onslaught was prolonged and the monasteries, unable to offer any effective resistance, declined in personnel, in wealth and in importance. The Norse invasion was finally overcome when the forces of King Brian Boruma defeated them at Clontarf though King Brian himself was killed.

Despite these two and a half centuries of attrition, Celtic monastic life survived, although impoverished and disorganised. There is evidence to suggest that the Benedictine rule was adopted in some Celtic monasteries, Jerpoint,[2] Erenagh,[3] St Mary's Abbey, Dublin,[4] Holy Cross,[5] Monas-tereven,[6] Fermoy,[7] Kilcooley[8] and Cashel.[9] Nevertheless the Benedictine movement did not make a great impact on Irish monasticism and at the time of the introduction of the Canons Regular of St Augustine and the Cistercian foundations, those communities still in existence willingly transferred their allegiance to the Augustinian and Cistercian rules.

Irish monasticism was often of a severe type and the Cistercian Order probably approximated nearest to what the native Irish considered the more perfect form of monasticism, having much in common with the traditional Irish system. On the other hand, the majority of religious men of the twelfth century might find the Cistercian Order too severe for themselves and the only alternative was the Canons Regular of St Augustine. As already mentioned, the Benedictines never really took root in Ireland and only one foundation of Carthusians[10] was established here. The only two forms of religious life at that period were those of the monks and the Canons. This gave an impetus to the Augustinian and Cistercian foundations during the twelfth century. Almost half of the Augustinian foundations — thirty-eight out of ninety-six Abbeys — were of the transferred Celtic personnel type and eight of the thirty-four Cistercian Abbeys were of the Celtic-Benedictine type.

*The bridge at Graignamanagh with Duiske Abbey
in the background.*

The Arrival of the Cistercians

St Malachy must have reflected on and studied with great anxiety the decline of Celtic monasticism. Some 211 Celtic monastic sites have been recorded.[1] By the twelfth century, however, many monasteries were deserted and others declined in personnel. St Malachy went to France to visit St Bernard; in fact he thought that he would like to become a Cistercian monk himself. St Malachy was very impressed with the Cistercian life and decided that he would like to introduce Cistercian monasticism into Ireland. St Bernard was delighted and agreed to train some Irish postulants who would later return to Ireland. In Letter 66 we have St Bernard's words to St Malachy: 'Go and with the wisdom given to you, prepare a site similar to what you have seen far removed from the turmoil of the world.'[2]

St Bernard was referring to a marsh area along a river bank. In the marsh bulrushes grew; the French word for this is Cistel and hence the place was called Cisteaux-Citeau.

When the Irish postulants were trained, they, accompanied by French monks, came to Ireland. They chose a site on the Mattock River, tributary to the River Boyne, and named this Mellifont Abbey. The Mellifont foundation was a success and in turn founded twenty-five daughter houses, nine of which were established before the Norman invasion took place.

St Malachy was very anxious to renew church life in Ireland. Indirectly he was assisted in this plan by the internal organisation of the Cistercian Order. In 1116 the Englishman Stephen Harding had drafted legislation to regulate the Order. He did not favour the Cluniac system wherein all the Abbeys formed one scattered family. He preferred that each Cistercian Abbey should be independent, that it should have a complete control over its temporal possessions and that filial relations between monasteries should exist.

Abbot Stephen explained his ideas to the four senior Abbots of Citeau. Each monastery, as he envisaged it, constituted a distinct family presided over by an Abbot irremovable by higher authority. In other words, once an Abbot was elected he was elected for life. Abbot Stephen united all the families into one Order. This system became known as the Charter of Charity. It was also laid down that each year the Abbot of a mother house should visit his daughter house to check on religious fervour and administration. At the annual General Chapter Meeting attended by the Abbot of each house, decisions regarding monastic life were made. As the land belonging to monasteries expanded, St Alberic the second Abbot of Citeau, saw the need for lay brothers (*Conversus*) and introduced them into the system. The Cistercians were anxious to adhere as far as possible to the Rule of St Benedict and in order to regulate the daily life of the monk, St Stephen Harding composed the Book of Usages.

The Rule of St Benedict requires that the whole of the Psalter should be recited weekly. In order to accomplish this, the monks had service in the Church seven times a day for a week. Feast days that would interrupt the weekly recitation had to be excluded from the Cistercian Calendar. The nocturnal or first of these services was at two o'clock in the morning. Matins or Prime was at 6 am, Tierce at 9 am, Sext at 12 noon, None at 3 pm, Vespers at 6 pm and Compline at 8 pm. The remainder of the day was taken up by manual labour and the *lectio divina*, the study of spiritual works. The Cistercians worked a sixteen hour day with only eight hours rest. This custom still prevails. Those of us who have visited Mount Mellerey, Roscrea, Mellifont, Moone or Bethlehem Abbey, Portglenone, have seen this daily monastic routine in practice.

Plan of the Abbey 1892

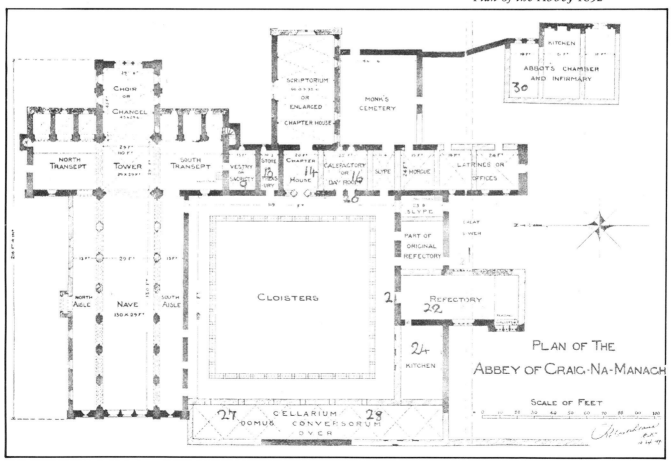

The Abbey's Charter

In order to place in perspective the foundation of Duiske Abbey, some thought must be given to what the charters call the 'Abbey of Ossory' and the 'Abbot of Ossory' and where the 'Abbey of Ossory' was situated. The 'Abbey of Ossory' was a Celtic one, and one would naturally expect that within the Celtic system the territory of Ossory would be the monastic Fine of such a person. Even the Charters are not clear on this, Duiske Abbey is spoken of as being 'in Ossory' but the parish of Graignamanagh as being in Leighlin. The 'Ossory' of the medieval Charters was not co-extensive with the Ossory Diocese today.

It is possible and probable that the 'Abbey of Ossory' was in Kilkenny and it was founded by Donal Mac Gillapatrick (who was killed in 1165).[1] The smaller Abbey of Killenny was made a daughter house of Ossory.[2] In 1180 Felix Dulaney was 'Abbot of Ossory' and this would indicate the survival of a Celtic community as described in the first chapter. As mentioned in the second chapter some Celtic Abbeys tried to renew their monastic observance by adopting the Benedictine Rule and this 'Abbey of Ossory' appears to have made arrangements regarding this.[3] Accordingly in 1180 when Killenny came under the aegis of 'The Abbey of Ossory' they all moved down to Jerpoint. However, at Jerpoint the community decided to become Cistercian and was made a daughter house of Baltinglass.[4] Another Celtic community Kilcooley, did

the same and was also made a daughter house of Baltinglass.[5]

These points are shown in the charters. It is obvious that good relations existed between the Irish Chief of Idrone, Dermot O'Ryan, and the Celtic 'Abbey of Ossory'. To the 'Abbot of Ossory' Dermot had, between 1162 and 1177, given a tract of land for the foundation of an Abbey. This charter is lost, but a confirmation charter exists. This foundation grant was intended as Benedictine as mentioned in the Charter:-

> Dermod, King of the Leinstermen *confirms* under his Seal the donation of lands made by Dermod Ua Rian, Chief of Idrone to Felix, 'Abbot of Ossory' for the construction of a monastery in honour of the Blessed Virgin Mary and St. Benedict... etc (circa 1162-1177).

Here the words 'St Benedict' indicate a Benedictine foundation.[6]

Furthermore this land was given in pure free and perpetual alms. This was fortunate and necessary, as otherwise with the advent of a new King, the Abbot would have had to pay a sum of money for the renewal of his Charter and between the death of an Abbot and the enthronement of his successor, the Abbey revenues would have been given over to the King.

However, this tract of land lay for forty years

without any effort being made to build an Abbey. Perhaps the 'Abbot of Ossory' with his house move to Jerpoint, with his transfer to the Cistercian Order and with affairs relating to the house at Killenny, could not spare or support monks for a new foundation. Furthermore the Irish Chief no longer ruled, the Normans were the new masters in south east Ireland. Nevertheless the latter were well disposed to the Cistercians, and under their patronage nine Cistercian houses were established in Ireland.

Strongbow, after conquering Ireland, married the daughter of the man with whom he fought, McMurrough's daughter Eva. Eva and Strongbow had one daughter Isabella, who married one of Strongbow's Lieutenants — William Marshal, later known as the Earl Marshal. William wanted to thank God for his success and decided to establish a Cistercian monastery in his fief on the west side of the River Barrow. He discussed this with another Norman, Philip de Prendergast. The latter was the son of Maurice de Prendergast, from the Flemish colony in Pembrokeshire, who had been granted land near Wexford by Strongbow.[7] Philip married Matilda de Quency and became lord of the manor of Enniscorthy.[8] This family of Prendergast, as we shall see, became very important in Graignamanagh.

Philip de Prendergast knew about this idle tract of land designated for a Benedictine monastery forty years previously by the Irish Chief Dermot. William Marshal made a petition to the General Chapter about building this Abbey. The General Chapter commissioned the Abbot of Dublin to act with the Abbot of Mellifont with regard to his petition to establish an Abbey.[9] Nothing happened and in 1201 the matter was brought before the General Chapter for a second time and the Abbots of Kilcooly and Jerpoint were commissioned to notify the Abbots of Mellifont and Dublin of the mandate of the General Chapter. The Abbots of Mellifont and Dublin were instructed to make diligent and solicitous enquiries regarding the possessions, the place chosen, and the wishes of the Earl, and having considered these matters to communicate the result of their deliberations to the Chapter.[10] The Abbots of Mellifont and Dublin did not in fact carry out their commission but the fault does not appear to have been theirs, for a statute of the Chapter of 1202 imposes a penance on the Abbots of Kilcooly and Jerpoint for failing to announce to the Abbots concerned the commission of the General Chapter regarding the proposed foundation by the Earl William Marshal. As a punishment for their remissness the two Abbots were ordered to remain outside their Abbatial stall for forty days and to perform for three days the penance laid down by the Rule for light faults, while they were to fast on bread and water for one of the three days.[11]

The matter of the foundation came before the General Chapter again in 1203 and this time the Abbots of Dunbrody and Stoquella were commissioned to go to the proposed site and have it examined, to report to the following Chapter the result of their investigations.[12] Here the word 'Stoquella' is a puzzle and should be interpreted as Stanley in Wiltshire, England.

Philip de Prendergast negotiated with the Abbot of Stanley about the possibility of a Norman Cistercian foundation in Ireland. The latter was delighted and agreed to send a colony of thirteen monks from Wiltshire to this foundation. In the meantime, William the Marshal, who had not yet arrived to take up his fief (in fact he did not come until 1207), decided to issue a new foundation Charter (1202) to supersede the O'Rian Charter. The new Charter stated: 'William Mariscalt, Earl of Pembroke, for the love of God, the salvation of his

Soul and that of his wife Isabel, and the Souls of their children and all the predecessors, founded in honour of the Blessed Virgin Mary, the Abbey of St Saviour of the Order of Cistercian monks in the lands of Dowiskyr... etc.'[13] This time, reference to St Benedict is omitted.

Jerpoint did not like the idea, as legally under the Irish Charter the tract of land belonged to her. She seemed to tolerate the layman called Fitz Robert holding it but probably knew that a Charter for a monastic foundation in perpetual alms implied that she would never regain it. The new Charter only affirmed a Norman confiscation. This dislike is shown in the language of the Abbots of Jerpoint and Killenny: 'ut in terra Ua Dauiskir Suam Construant abbatiam'[14] — such was the terms of their concession to their new neighbours and rivals. The General Chapter agreed to the foundation of the Abbey as well, but the proper procedure for this had not been carried out by the Abbot of Stanley. He had not waited for final approval by the General Chapter. The latter had gone ahead and sent an Abbot and community to Ireland despite the prohibition of the Father Abbot. As a result of this action the Abbot of Stanley was deposed in 1204. 'Depositus est R. Abbas Stanlegh a Capituto Cistercianse eoquod duxent conventum in Hibernian absque licentia capituli.'[15] Nevertheless his demotion did not last very long, because in the following year he was elected Abbot of Buckfast in Devon and the Norman Cistercian foundation of Duiske proceeded.

As has been mentioned, when the Abbot of Stanley was approached by Philip de Prendergast to send a colony of monks to Ireland he did so immediately. On 21 July, the Abbot, Thomas Rokby, Robert Nottingham, Piers Geneville, Geoffry Comyn, Gilbert Shorthall and Walter de Valle sailed from Bristol. On the second day a strong wind blew against them and their boat lost a top sail, but they managed after a six day crossing to reach the Quay of Ross.[16] Once they reached Ireland they decided to travel on foot rather than by boat along the river. At Rosbercon they engaged the help of a family called O'Ryan. The latter had three gillies and two boys with panniers and cleaves, into which they placed their tools, pots, blankets and Abbot's Box. The guides led them through the woods of the Rower and halted when they reached Loughmerans[17] near the city of Kilkenny. This was part of the farm belonging to the Earl Marshal's Castle Estate. However, the monks decided that this site was not suitable and went to Annamult.[18] On the night of their journey to Annamult they stayed with the Abbot of Jerpoint, giving him a wool sack as a friendly gesture.

The monks knew that they could not stay at Annamult because on the opposite bank of the river were the lands of Jerpoint. The Cistercian regulations laid down that they must be ten Burgundian leagues from another house. Nevertheless Annamult provided a pioneering site until they found a more suitable place.

The monks' next move was to cross the River Nore, move east and make for the Bearna Mor Copponagh. When they reached the gap they looked down and before them lay the Vale of Duiske on the edge of the Leinster granite and a well wooded valley. They proceeded to within one mile of the confluence of the Duiske and the Barrow and encountered an Irish village, at which McMurrough had begun to build an Irish Church which was never finished. This was in Grange townland.

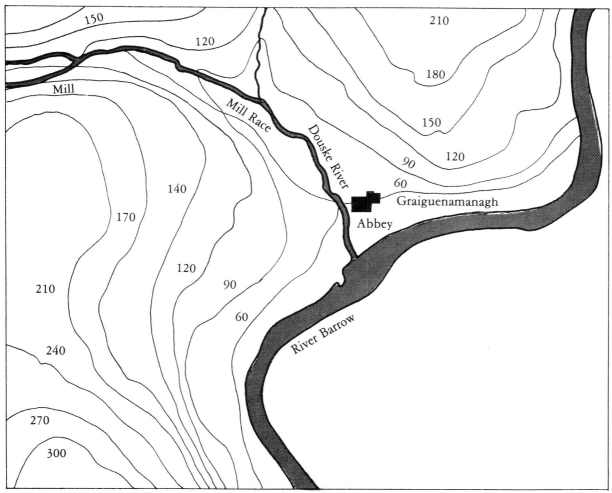

150

120

Mill

Mill Race

Douske River

210

180

150

120

90

60

Graiguenamanagh

Abbey

140

170

120

90

60

210

240

270

300

River Barrow

The Site of Duiske Abbey

Splendid Restraint

Medieval Cistercian monasteries were built to a uniform plan. The monastery was constructed in the form of a quadrangle around an open space, the Church being on the north side. Surrounding this central space was the cloister, an arcaded gallery with a lean-to roof. The northern walk of the cloister, facing the sun and sheltered by the massive Church building which generally extended the length of the nave of the Church as far as the south transept, was provided with benches for reading and was called the reading cloister. This was 130 feet long and 39 feet wide. The eastern walk extended southwards from the angle of the nave and the southern transept along the entire length of the eastern range of the buildings. Nearest to the Church was the Sacristy, 15 feet by 24 feet — in Duiske this was vaulted and lighted by a window in the east. Then came the Library [14] and the Chapter House. The Chapter House in Duiske Abbey was 24 feet by 20 feet and had a large doorway opening into the Cloisters, with two side lights also. This would have left almost all of the west end wall of the Chapter room open. In the centre was a column, which carried the roof and in Duiske this was highly ornamented. Next to the Chapter House was the Parlour, [16] where the monks engaged in necessary conversation with their superior, and the Scriptorium or community room. This was not planned as part of the original building, being more of an afterthought. It measured 66 feet by

33 ½ feet and was reached via a doorway in the east wall of the Chapter room, at a place where the Abbot's stone seat would have been placed. In Duiske Abbey the Scriptorium door opens to the north instead of the west. The Scriptorium is usually over the Chapter room, but here it acts as a vestibule to the Chapter room.

The monk's dormitory was generally located on the first floor over the whole eastern range and was connected directly with the Church by a staircase known as the night stairs, since it was used by the monks for the purpose of coming from the dormitory to the Church for the night office. The monks were the first people in Ireland to sleep upstairs. The regulation in St. Bernard's own monastery of Clairvaux was that the monks should sleep in a dormitory in which there was a double row of couches, with each monk being alloted a space breadthwise of six feet. According to this regulation Duiske Abbey had accommodation for fifty-four monks and sixty lay brothers. I cannot find any larger than this in Ireland.

Turning west at the end of the eastern cloister one found oneself in the southern cloister which ran alongside the southern range of the monastic buildings. This range contained the calefactory, 25 feet by 24 feet, [22] or warming room at its eastern end, the refectory or dining hall of the monks, generally known as the Frater, in the centre and the kitchen at the western end. Opposite the door of

Numbers 14, 16 and 22 refer to the Map on page 16.

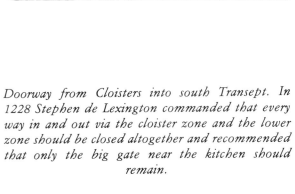

Doorway from Cloisters into south Transept. In 1228 Stephen de Lexington commanded that every way in and out via the cloister zone and the lower zone should be closed altogether and recommended that only the big gate near the kitchen should remain.

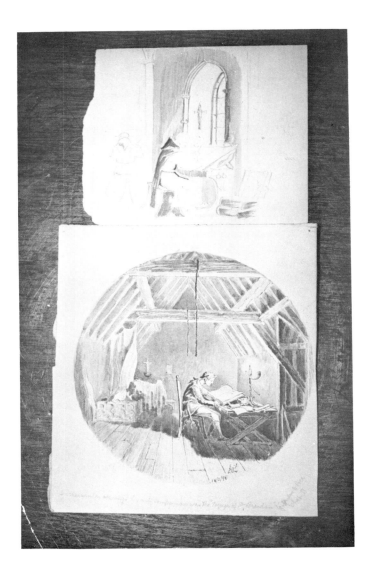

Pen and ink drawings. The top drawing depicts a monk at work in the Scriptorium. The bottom drawing depicts a novice studying. (J O'Leary.)

the refectory was located the Lavabo 23 which opened out of the cloister. Here was the fountain at which the brethren washed their hands before entering the refectory for meals.

The west range of the monastery extended from the Church to the kitchen on the south. This range included the Domus Conversorum while their dormitory was overhead. [27] [28] The southern half of the Domus Conversorum formed the Refectory of the conversi on the ground floor. Other than the main cloistral area there was often a second set of buildings always physically removed from these, sometimes termed the Camera of the Abbot. These buildings contained the Abbot's house, the guest house, the infirmary and were sometimes termed the Lower Zone.

Within the monastery the main building was the Church, the *raison d'être* of any community. Wolfgang Brunfels points out that draughtsmen always conceived of the whole monastery as a unity, a unity that found its completion in the worship to which the style and layout of the building was directed. The detailed measurements were the fruits of deeply considered planning, so that the higher a building rose the greater the demand for clear-cut lines and proportions in its shaping.[1] When we consider the cathedral-like dimensions of Duiske Abbey then we must reflect on the skill of its architects in the Middle Ages. The module supplied by the Church Crossing, 29 feet by 29 feet, governs not only the dimensions of the Church but also of those of the buildings around the cloister and the cloister itself.

According to Braun, the plan of these Medieval Monasteries mentioned above depended to a fundamental degree upon the principle of design by bays. Each elevation was a repetition of a series of bays individually designed but placed end to end to achieve the whole. Each bay had to be considered

Numbers 23, 27 and 28 refer to the map on page 23.

Mullions of the former Cistercian refectory window at reading gallery level.
Today this is a workshop belonging to C O'Leary, a resident in the former Cloisters.

Interior view of the Rose Window after restoration in the south transept.

both with regard to its plan on the ground and to how its proportions became affected as the structure rose. For a bay is a unit of building, not an elevational unit; its elevational presentation is an aesthetic exercise which followed the acceptance of its structural suitability. He illustrates this by describing the system of vaulting: 'the construction of vaulting is very much simplified if the bay over which it is thrown be made square, so that the curvature of the opposed transverse arches forming the vault have the same radius. Thus the eleventh century aisle is usually set out as a series of square bays with each arch of the main arcade equal to the width of the aisle.'[2] These proportions are beautifully illustrated in Duiske Abbey. One has only to look at the seven arches of the aisle to appreciate this concept.

A cathedral in length.

The unit employed in setting out was the pole — literally a pole. There was no national standard of length. The surveyors who built these abbeys could not multiply two by two without the use of a chequer board, for Arabic numerals were three centuries away. It has been said that each master builder cut his own pole and in so doing varied the interpretation of the linear foot.[3] It has also been said that a random length of the feet of sixteen men placed one behind the other was used as standard length. This was a foundation being established from England so it is possible that similar methods were used here. Thus the size of Abbey Churches could have been fortuitously related to the length of the pole selected by the surveyor — or perhaps the surveyor, in making his selection of a pole of certain length, may have been guided by a maximum size of the abbey plan based on the cost of project. Nevertheless the fact that the Cistercians demanded strict uniformity in their monasteries and that the layout of the Cistercian monastery was determined by a standard plan to which all houses were supposed to adhere makes it most unlikely that the size of the Abbey Church was fortuitously related to the size of the pole adopted by the surveyor for it is certain that monastic architects well acquainted with the Cistercian plan took charge of the building operations in new foundations and it is at least very probable that these architects used a pole of standard length. In the case of two foundations made from Clairvaux we have definite evidence that the plans were brought from the mother house by a builder monk. These two foundations were Mellifont Abbey in Ireland, to which St. Bernard himself sent from Clairvaux the French monk Robert[4] to supervise the building of the new monastery, and Fountains in England, the plans of which were brought from Clairvaux by a famous builder monk Geoffrey d'Alaine.[5] The

A corner decoration in the Baptistry.

Corbel found amongst masonry which had been incorporated in rubble blocking up a window in the choir.

plans for Duiske Abbey were brought from the Abbey of Strata Florida by John St Aubyn, the Welsh monk.[6] According to the Annals of Duiske he was sometimes called 'the builder who brought with him the building chart and a troop of marvellously skilled craftsmen to help the native masons at the carved work and tiling'.[7] An examination and comparison of the plans of Duiske Abbey with that of Strata Florida shows how almost equal in size they were: the nave of Duiske Abbey Church was 130 feet by 39 feet, that of Strata Florida 128 feet 6 inches by 28 feet; the width of

A doorway in Duiske Abbey, Graignamanagh.

the aisle of Duiske was 13 feet, that of Strata Florida 12 feet 6 inches; the square of the lantern tower of Duiske was 29 feet, that of Strata Florida 28 feet; the breadth across the transepts of Duiske was 110 feet, that of Strata Florida 117 feet 3 inches, and the choir of Duiske Abbey was 45 feet by 29 feet 6 inches, whilst that of Strata Florida was 52 feet 6 inches by 28 feet. Each abbey had seven arches separating the nave from the aisles. With such similar measurements one can claim that the Cistercian ideal of uniformity was adhered to in Duiske. [8]

Cistercian abbeys were forbidden to have elaborate carvings, although in some Irish Cistercian Abbeys, particularly in the West of Ireland, such as Boyle, Knockmoy and Corcumroe, this is displayed. Sometimes the Cistercians had to accept elaborate carving as a gesture of a wealthy benefactor such as Crobhdearg O Connor of Connaught. However the splendour of Duiske Abbey is in its restraint; elaborate carvings are not present. The mouldings consist for the most part of rounds and fillets, very simple but effective, and the work of men who knew how to restrain their artistic expression rather than give free rein to their ideas. Is an arc or Gothic arch not more difficult to carve than foliage. Each voussoir of the ninety-six voussoirs of the arch are of light and dark contrasts and have nine rounds and eight fillets. The blocks forming the interior of the window casements were pointed with red pigment to accentuate them. Today this red pigment can be seen in the window of the south transept. A photograph of a Wilson drawing published in the Irish Builder February 1876 shows this to be a characteristic of Duiske and a typical architectural practice often found in Cistercian abbeys in Europe. The piers have the angles chamfered at the base; the chamfer is stopped at the springing of the arch by a simple leaf design and from this springs the arch moulding; no capital is employed in this arrangement. The only capitals are in the corbel shafts in the thickness of the piers which have early English Capitals with dog tooth ornament and

Making an Arch Hood during restoration

Splendid Result: Notice the alternate light and dark voussoirs — Creativity and a play on contrast.

foliage carving. This dog tooth chevron pattern is seen in the cusped processional doorway. The appreciative eye will linger at the delicately chiselled masons' marks on its jambs. Who but a Norman could have made and designed the staircase to the Octagonal tower in the north east angle of the north transept which was formed in the thickness of the east wall of the transept? Each step was carved like a keyhole, eight inches deep by two foot ten inches wide, the circumference of the shaft measuring two foot. On every alternate step is a finger hold. One must admire the Norman skill that could place such a staircase in the thickness of a wall. This must have been well thought out and planned beforehand. Perhaps as the science of metrology advances and Medieval architecture receives the study, attention and restoration that it deserves we will come to appreciate the balance and proportion found in the Abbey buildings of Cistercian Duiske.

Entrance to keyhole shaped staircase

Close up of stone staircase to Tower.

Building the Abbey

There were thirty four Cistercian Abbeys in Medieval Ireland. Twenty five of these were in river valleys, Abbeydorney was on an island in a bog, Inch was on a drumlin and the remaining seven, Assaroe, Abbeymahon, Dunbrody, Tintern, Dublin, Middleton and Corcumroe might be described as coastal. The term river valley here denotes a general rather than a specific situation. Abbeys in river valleys drew certain advantages from this type of location such as accessibility, availability of water for domestic needs and a power supply, possibilities for fishing and the prospect of water meadows. The precise siting of abbeys within a valley was determined not only by a potentially greater facility for using the water at any given point, but also by other considerations such as the presence of a solid foundation on which to build, a feature by no means ubiquitous in river valleys. Generally Cistercian abbeys in Ireland were built as near to water as possible on a solid foundation which was necessarily above flood level. Hence low river terraces where rock was near the surface were especially favoured. Nevertheless, there was a hierarchy of siting values, namely, water requirements, solid foundations, and building stone.

All Cistercian Abbeys needed water for two purposes: for domestic use and for power. A good domestic water supply was essential to an abbey. Monasteries were spacious buildings planned to accommodate large and active communities. The abbey's life-line was the abbey stream. This was usually an artificial water course cut from some nearby stream for the benefit of the monastery alone. Cistercian abbeys were, as already described, built to a standard plan which was based on the assumption that an artificial water course could be engineered, passing first of all along the southern side of the claustral complex and if possible flowing from west to east, so as to pass the refectory and kitchen before reaching the rear dorter at the end of the monk's house. Therefore, in order to accommodate the standard plan, the engineering of the Great Sewer and the water conduits demanded that the site should have a north-west to south-east slope. This resulted in twenty-five out of thirty-four Cistercian Abbeys in Ireland being situated on the right banks of rivers, and Graignamanagh Abbey was no exception. Ancillary to the advantage of the site having a north-west to south-east slope was the ease with which the abbey stream could be carried through the offices of the abbey in buried conduits to flush and well up in those parts of the abbey where it was needed, and then, having fulfilled its appointed task, to return to the river.

Water for power was essential for Medieval Abbeys. The most desirable water power situation was one where a tributary stream with a relatively steep gradient joined a main river as at Graignamanagh where the Duiske River joins the River Barrow, an ideal site for the mills of Duiske.

The Great Drain, the Main Sewer of Duiske Abbey. This section was photographed in Colm O'Leary's yard.

Note the Norman arch, four feet wide and six feet high.

Evidence of the ancient water system is seen in an underground passage running the entire breadth of the Abbey from east to west; it is about four feet wide and six feet high and was arched. It is now filled with earth and in some places the arch is broken away. The Great Drain was discovered when foundations were being dug for the installation of baking ovens for a man called O'Leary in 1819.

Horizontal view of the same conduit. Often such conduits have been described as escape tunnels but this was not their function.

The next requirement for building an abbey was a suitable building stone. For Graignamanagh the stone used was the local granite and shale of the district. However, before the abbey could be built a quarry had to be opened. On the opening of the quarry the first thing that was generally necessary was to clear away the over-burden of earth. Moreover when the top layer of stone was reached it was almost always of inferior quality, being fissured and unsuitable for cutting into blocks, though useful as random rubble and infilling for walls. However, lifting gear and tackle limited the depth of quarrying in the Middle Ages. Old quarries in close proximity to monastic sites were seldom more than thirty feet deep. The stone for Duiske Abbey was quarried from the area now known as the Fair Green: here large irregular sized granite boulders were obtained, and some were also quarried at Killeen. Sand for mortar may have come from Tinnahinch; the present Road to Borris runs through this deposit.

Various methods were used, depending on the quality of the stone for building a monastery. Medieval abbeys involved the raising of a thick wall. Three examples may be adduced: the random core rubble type which consisted of using a comparatively thin shell of solid masonry which was filled in with a mass or core of rubble and stone chippings compacted with mortar, blocks of irregular size and shape compacted with mortar into a solid mass about four feet wide, and large blocks of hewn sandstone approximately two feet by three feet as at Boyle Abbey, Co Roscommon. It was the second of these methods — irregular granite blocks compacted with mortar — that was used at Duiske. However, the irregular size of the blocks necessitated the insertion of a horizontal slate course every eighteen inches, as the building rose. Such slate was easily split, but the edges had to be smoothed and sawn and trimmed to give a smooth outward appearance. This use of a slate course at intervals was also used at Kells, Co Kilkenny and the quarry from which the Augustinians quarried the slate was at Mealoughmore. The source of the slate for Duiske Abbey may have been the Flag Mount quarries. This was an innovation, for many of the early Irish monasteries used a damp-proof course of cow dung.

Obviously such ragged walls needed an attractive material for dressing the building, the arches, the windows, the doors and all major openings. Granite and rubble did not have the finished solid and pleasing appearance of blocked limestone. Furthermore in the area formerly known as the Pale there is hardly a single ecclesiastical building that is not dressed with sandstone because the Normans did not like to work with the local hard limestone. They preferred to work with oolitic limestone and early evidence shows that they imported this from Bristol. The Abbey of Stanley, mother house of Duiske, was built with excellent quality Bath oolite from Hazelbury in Box Parish. The monks had a quarry there before 1241, but in that year upon the Feast of St John ante Portam Lateran, 'Robert Abbot of Stanley in Wiltshire and the convent of the same place give to the said convent (of Lacock) one part of their quarry of Haslebury being in length 76 feet and in width that which was theirs, that they may take as much stone from the place in exchange for the other quarry that the convent (of Lacock) bought of Henry brok.'[1]

At the time of this arrangement (c. 1241) Duiske Abbey was still being built, although we have no record of the movement of stone to Ireland at this time. However, according to the researches of D M Waterman[2] the oolite stone used was obtained from the Dundry quarries near Bristol, four miles south of the River Avon. The quarries of Dundry Hill were let on lease by the Bishop of Bath and

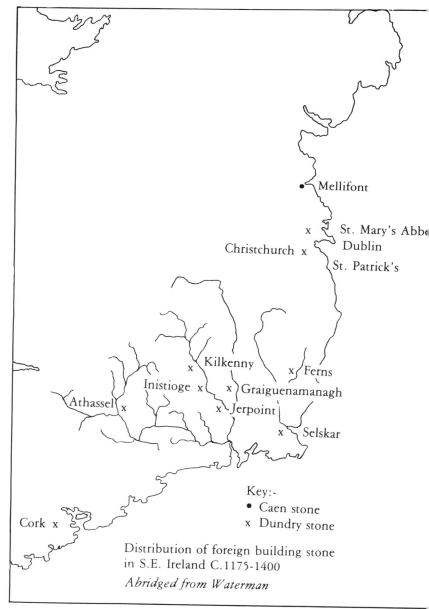

Mellifont

St. Mary's Abbe

Christchurch x

Dublin

St. Patrick's

Kilkenny

Ferns

Inistioge x

Graiguenamanagh

Athassel x

Jerpoint

Selskar

Cork x

Key:-
• Caen stone
x Dundry stone

Distribution of foreign building stone in S.E. Ireland C.1175-1400
Abridged from Waterman

Wells and between 1491-1512 were rented by St Augustine's Abbey (later the Cathedral in Bristol) to provide stone for Abbot Newland's additions.[3] The position of Bristol on the tidal River Avon ensured easy water-borne transport for the output of the Dundry quarries either as a building stone or for monumental sculpture. This freestone in blocks 3 feet by 1 foot by 1 foot[4] was brought to the port of Dublin to become the dressed stone-work of Christ Church Cathedral. Some imported oolite was brought up the River Barrow to the slipway of Graignamanagh 'and many a Kerne came from his fastness to view the clarachwans, flat bottomed boats, from Ross as they drew up the abbey slip laden with rich glass, stone and various marbles for the Chapter house', but whether this refers to the oolite stone brought from the Stanley Abbey quarry c. 1241 at a time when Duiske was being built or from the Augustinian quarry c. 1491 is not known. However the date 1491 is late in the history of building operations in Duiske Abbey and it may be reasonably presumed that Duiske Abbey imported oolite from the quarries of her mother house c. 1241.

The Dundry stone was used extensively for the dressed work of Duiske Abbey and can still be seen in the three western bays of the nave, the sacristy and the dorter[5] (dormitory). In the fourteenth century Purbeck marble was sent across the Irish Sea to some abbeys. This stone was kept in small pieces and was used in the famous marble tree of Duiske. According to Comerford the Chapter House was the most elaborately ornamented apartment in the Abbey.[6] It was a room 24 feet by 20 feet and opened upon the cloisters through a large Gothic arch containing within it three smaller arches of blue marble beautifully carved. Another arch on the opposite side led to the library. Of the great central column nothing but the foundation remains. This pillar, spoken of by the older inhabitants as the Marble Tree stood some eight feet high from the base to the capital whence the branches spread to meet the corresponding ribs of the groined roof. It is described as having been marvellously beautiful, enriched with carving of the twelve Apostles, festoons of vine branches etc. The beauty of the carving tempted unscrupulous visitors to carry away stone after stone until nothing now remains but a few of the corbels from which the arches sprang. It is related that in about 1816 the Marble Tree was presented by a Mr. Cheevers[7] to a friend in Carlow who had it carried away at night and set up as an arrangement in his garden at Somerton. However, it is now claimed that the last remaining portions were incorporated in the Roman Catholic Church of Graigcullen.

All this imported stone for the lavish embellishment of Duiske Abbey suggests prosperity and the dependence on water-borne transport in the Middle Ages. The inclusion of foreign building stone may have been due to the wealth of the Abbey, or to the whim of a generous benefactor, or it may have been simply a cultural preference of the Normans for this stone. The Norman taste is seen in the Abbey's architecture. Duiske Abbey was sufficiently wealthy to keep in line with architectural developments. In the Norman areas of Ireland the architectural style was either Norman or English transitional.

Duiske Abbey was very fortunate to have a man called Hugh le Rous to witness her Charter. It is believed that the latter introduced Norman style architecture into Ireland. Hugh le Rous became an Augustinian Canon and Prior of Kells Abbey, Co Kilkenny, and was later made Bishop of Ossory. Hugh le Rous never lost interest in the Cistercian Abbey of Duiske: we find him giving the village of Stathmarkestawan (Ti-Kerlevan), together with its churches, to the Church of St Mary of the Abbey of

Duiske, reserving yearly to the Mother Church of Ossory 20 shillings in 'lieu of all services and exactions whatsoever'. One notices here also the Welsh ecclesiastical organisational practice of having 'Mother Churches'.

Building operations were slow in Medieval days. A time study carried out by three masons restoring Holy Cross Abbey in 1974, showed that a mason using the medieval tools of comb, pitchure, chisel, hammer, punch, could dress only three blocks of hewn limestone per day. To trim and saw the slate rocks for Duiske must have taken longer and must have required the services of a large number of masons. The Normans built abbeys of vast dimensions and Duiske was one of the largest in Europe. No wonder the Great Church took twenty years to build. In 1228, Stephen de Lexington ordered the cellarer to supply enough lead to put a roof on the Northern part of the church, and at various times the building programme was supported by Hugh le Rous' successors. Thus we have Peter Manessin who 'confirmed to St Saviour's the Church of Tullachany with all its appurtenances and all the tithes of his own grange reserving thereout a mark yearly to the Church of Kilkenny payable after the death of Hugh, the Dean[10] he also, confirmed to this abbey the Church of Athermolt[11] Tullachany was chargeable with the aforesaid mark'. In 1243, Bishop John St John made his donation to the Abbey and gave the lands of Killary to it, reserving to himself and his successors the yearly rent of 10 shillings.[12] It must be noticed that these donations coincided with the most active building period of the Abbey.

One of the great legacies of Duiske Abbey is a speciality of the Medieval Cistercian period. This is the tiled floor. Like its Mother House, Stanley, Duiske had one. Of the thirty-four Cistercian Abbeys in Medieval Ireland tiles have only been found in Mellifont Abbey and Duiske. It has been

Cistercian wheel pattern tiles. Note the fleur-de-lys and the shamrock: the assimilation and reconciliation of men of Irish and Norman culture in Duiske Abbey.

estimated that some forty-two patterns of Cistercian tiles exist. The patterns have been described as mainly wheel or rose designs. The wheel patterns were usually set in a square base and often the tile patterns were the same as in the rose windows. The patterns were cut out in templates of leather, pressed into hard clay. Five colours of tiles were usual: green, yellow, white, brown and black. Sometimes the tiles had a legend on them; those at Mellifont Abbey had 'Ave Maria'. The Mellifont tiles were imported from Fountains; Jervaux Abbey,

England imported her tiles from France and it is likely that the tiles of Duiske Abbey were imported from Stanley, Wiltshire. However, the granitic texture of the tiles may suggest local clay. The Duiske Abbey tiles are in situ. An inspection area has been arranged and a demonstration area has been secured at the Baptistry Door. The Duiske tiles are of the wheel pattern type. Some have a legend but this cannot be fully obtained until the floor of the Church is fully excavated. The Duiske tiles are unusual and incorporate the Norman fleur-de-lys and the Irish Shamrock — a Norman house in Ireland, or a message for posterity — the assimilation and reconciliation of men of two cultures in one abbey. If the restoration work now in progress includes the lowering of the present floor level to the original one, it is likely that there will be a north-east-south-west slope on it, but this was typical of Cistercian Churches.

Tiles in situ — *inspection area in north transept of Medieval floor uncovered beneath six feet of rubble. All Cistercian Abbey floors sloped from NW to SE. When the Abbey Church was given to the people of Graignamanagh as a Parish Church there may have been a desire to level off the floor, hence the infilling.*

A castle on the Grange of Annamult, the second site occupied by the Cistercians before they came to Duiske.

The Monastic Estate

The Cistercians were primarily agriculturalists and resulting from this activity their landed estates grew up. It has already been mentioned that the monks first settled at Loughmeran about two miles north of Kilkenny on land belonging to William Marshal, Earl of Pembroke, but only remained there for a short time. They then removed to Annamult about six miles south of the city to a parcel of land bordered on the east by the River Nore and on the south by the King's River. Both these rivers flow in deeply incised valleys of Carboniferous limestone marking a 200 feet peneplain. The lowland itself is covered with limestone drifts in the form of hum-

mocky ground moraine interspersed with bogs where the drainage was interrupted and lakes or fens formed. Associated with these features is the presence of a large number of bogs, some very small and others covering several square miles, which have developed on a fen base between the ground moraine.

However at Annamult the Cistercians found themselves on the opposite bank of the river to Jerpoint and this was against the Statutes of the Order which necessitated that they should be ten Burgundian leagues from each other, so they could not build an abbey there. Then they acquired a new site

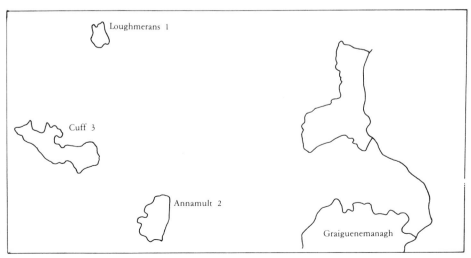

Map showing the basic relationship of the four sites.

Loughmerans 1

Cuff 3

Annamult 2

Graiguenemanagh

38

View from the top floor of the Castle at Annamult.

Vault in Castle at Annamult.

Stairway in walls of Annamult Castle.

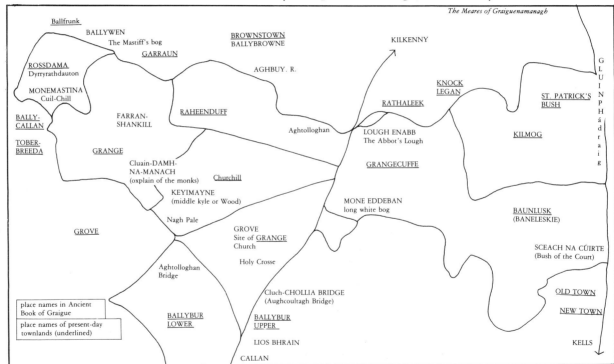

called Tulachany, which was later changed to Grange Castri and is now Grange in the barony of Shilleogher. This grange lay on the eastern slope of the Slieve Ardagh Hills which in turn slope gently down for more than thirty miles to the Nore Valley. Most of this lowland area is covered with limestone drift and is generally well drained and fertile. Details for the siting of this grange are excellent and are found in Nos 3 and 4 of the Abbey's

Charters.[1] Number 4 is the same as No 3 except that the words in No 3, 'terram quam Stephanus de Valle tenuit' are replaced by the more specific description, 'et Tullachani cum pertinenibus suis scillicet Clundaf et Kilmeggeth et Liscrithan'. This latter Charter was apparently re-written to obviate any future dispute as to the extents of the lands granted at Tulachany which constitute the modern parish of Grange, Co Kilkenny.

Auncient Book of Graige

Tulachany:- The third site chosen by the Cistercian monks, equating with the present day civil parish of Grange. The boundaries shown here are mentioned in the Ancient Book of Graigy. *In the medieval monastic period it was customary once a year for the Abbott to 'beat the bounds'. This meant he rode in a clockwise direction on the perimeter of his estate noting topographical features. A record of such a journey is noted in the Ancient Book' under the heading The Meares (ie the boundaries) of Grangtullaghan. This subsequent out farm (ie a Grange) of the medieval Tulleghan is equivalent to 1934 acres two roods, twenty-four perches in statute acres. In 1228 Stephen de Lexington ordered that the carpenter should be sent to this grange before the 1st November, and that the cobbler's shop should be changed from Duiske Abbey to this place we well.*

Cuffesgrange from the air, showing Grove Church ruins and Abbots' Lough (Lough Enabb) and Mone Eddeban (the long white bog).

The moat site of Grange Cuffe left of the Church in the middle foreground.

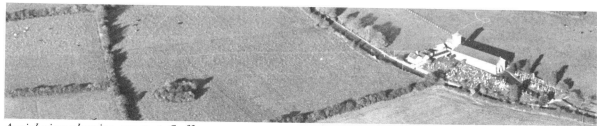

Aerial view showing moat at Cuffesgrange

From this site the Cistercians moved to their permanent site at Bun Duiske, Bun Dubhuisce on the western bank of the River Barrow. Additional grants of lands in the Tulachany area were made to the monks between 1221-1225 and these lands now form the parish of Grange consisting of the townlands of Grange, Grange Cuffe, Church Hill, Kilmog, Roheendus and Rossdama. The bulk of the Cistercian lands, however, show that not all the land contained in the parish formed part of the original endowment. The period between 1204-1280 was, generally speaking, a period of growth and by the end of that time the monks of Duiske had acquired all the possessions they held at the time of the dissolution of the Abbey more than three centuries later. The Charters of Duiske bear witness to the consolidation of existing monastic lands by the acquisition of new lands in the vicinity of lands already held by the monks and by the exchange of distant lands for lands nearer home which could be more easily consolidated and merged in existing granges. Most of the new lands were the gift of benefactors such as Bishop Hugh's grant of Tikerlevan near Coppanagh,[2] the gift of a church and land in Idrone and a chapel and land in Forth, both in Co Carlow (c. 1224) and the gift of three carucates of land in Rathboghall,[3] now Monksgrange in the barony of Bantry, Co Wexford, c. 1226. In one case, two carucates of land originally granted to the Benedictines of Glascarrig, Co Wexford,[4] were by

arrangement between the Abbot of Duiske and the Prior of Glascarrig transferred to Duiske in 1223. Here is another instance of Benedictine land being given to the Cistercians. In 1255 Pope Alexander IV allowed chapels on the granges since it was becoming more common for the monks to reside on them. The Cistercians were only inclined to furnish chapels on their more important granges. Since Grange Cuffe was also a former Abbey site, its temporary buildings became the grange buildings and the chapel may have been retained.

Now the question must be asked, 'What was a grange?' 'Grange' comes from the Latin *grangia*, a granary, and was in fact an outfarm of the Abbey. On this outfarm there was a residence for the monks who lived and worked there. The person in charge was a monk called a Grangarius and he was assisted by a number of lay brothers. In the early days the Cistercians did not say Mass on their granges and were obliged to return to the Abbey for Sunday Mass; later they were allowed to have small oratories on the granges. All the produce of the grange went directly to the Abbey; none of it was sold by the grange. To the Cistercians we accredit this new townland name in Ireland. Fortunately on the Grange of Annamult there are the remains of the residence of the monks of Duiske Abbey. One remembers that these monks were Norman French, hence the Brothers were *les frères*. Gradually 'the brother's barn' came to be known and passed into later day speech as the 'Friar's Barn', although it had nothing to do with the Mendicant Orders. The north, south and west walls of these are discernible and appear to have surrounded a central court yard 60 feet by 107 feet. The aforementioned walls are traceable, with six footholds in the north wall, twelve footholds in the west and eight in the south wall, and are approximately four feet thick. The Cistercians did not abandon the Annamult site, nor the Grange Cuffe site. Annamult was a residential site with a castle; Grange Cuffe was a moated grange. The moat is in Churchill townland and the chapel, 60 feet by 20 feet is also in this townland. The farm buildings were in Grange Cuffe townland as was the Abbot's lake or fish pond. These were well developed sites on good quality land and probably provisioned and sustained the work of those actually engaged in the building of the monastery on the River Duiske. The builder monks lived at Old Grange, one mile west of the Abbey. The building programme took a long time: the Church was ready in 1220, the cloisters in 1224, and the living accommodation about 1227. Whilst the monks were living in Annamult and Grange Cuffe, they recruited many monks and lay brothers, so many that when Stephen de Lexington came on a visitation to Ireland in 1228, he put a limit on the numbers. Only fifty-six monks and sixty lay brothers were permitted to live in the monastery. As we shall see in the following chapter, the Cistercians of Duiske Abbey had four granges which they retained up to 1541, namely Annamult, Cuffe's Grange, Killenny and Monks' Grange.

Monks' Grange, Co Wexford, was an upland grange (600 feet) on the slopes of the Blackstairs. The present owner of the Grange Demesne (T. Orpen Esq) has not found any evidence of former residential grange buildings, but his home may have been built on the site. Nevertheless at the rear

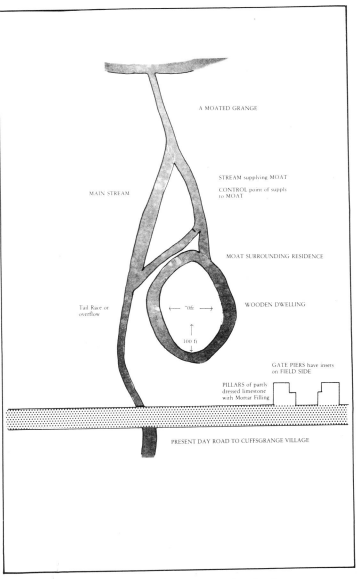

A MOATED GRANGE

STREAM supplying MOAT

CONTROL point of supply to MOAT

MAIN STREAM

MOAT SURROUNDING RESIDENCE

Tail Race or overflow

WOODEN DWELLING

←— 70ft —→

100 ft

GATE PIERS have insets on FIELD SIDE

PILLARS of partly dressed limestone with Mortar Filling

PRESENT DAY ROAD TO CUFFSGRANGE VILLAGE

This was Grange Castri or Castle Grange the third site developed by the Monks of Duiske Abbey

Inset pillars, one hundred yards from the moat.

Grove-Cuffesgrange. Notice moat and entrance in the foreground.

View taken from the top of the moat showing three courses for water: notice the tail race. This can be traced from the bush in the background to the moat.

of his house is a large pond, supplied by a well called Tobar na ġe (the well of the goose) and from this emerges a conduit flowing in the direction of his residence. This would suggest a reservoir-cum-fish pond and would be similar to Kilcooley Abbey's fish pond (Co Tipperary), also at an altitude of 600 feet which supplied that Abbey's needs. Thus Duiske Abbey had fish ponds at Killenny, Grange Cuffe, Cordredan and possibly at Monks' Grange, Co Wexford. On the other hand,

Mr Orpen has informed me (in conversation) that he has heard this referred to as the Baize Pond.

Baize (origin French) was a coarse woollen cloth, with a long nap, bay coloured. This brown coloured material would have been used for making the garments of the lay-brothers, who wore brown and not white like the monks. Such an interpretation would suggest that this was the pond in which the lay-brothers of this grange washed their habits.

Exterior view of Church ruins in Grove.

The Old Abbey

The Cistercians had another grange, the Grange of Shanavanister, alias old Abbey. This parcel of land was not originally intended as a grange, but as an abbey site.[1] This abbey called Killenny was intended as a daughter house of Jerpoint and Dermot O'Ryan, Chief of Idrone, granted these lands to Jerpoint for that purpose. Dermot O'Ryan's charter is not extant although there is preserved a precis and Inspeximus and Confirmation of it by one of his descendants two and a half centuries later. There is also a confirmation of it granted by Dermot Mac Murrough, King of Leinster.

Killenny Abbey was situated in the townland of Old Abbey, now Barrowmount in the Civil Parish of Grange Silvae in the diocese of Leighlin. On the ground traces of the ruins can be seen. Only a few of the lands granted by Dermot O'Ryan for the purpose of the new monastery can be identified. Dun inni is Doninga a townland in the parish of Grange Silvae: Druim ro is now Mount Loftus in the parish of Powerstown. According to the Annals of Loch Ce, John of Salernum, Papal legate, held a synod at Dublin in 1202.[2] This John of Salernum granted to Thomas Abbot of Killenny and his convent a charter confirming the monks in possession of their lands and giving them freedom from tithes, the right of electing their abbot and other privileges. In 1220[3] another grant was given to Killenny Abbey by Alan Beg. This grant was for 'an acre of land with the houses which the monks have posses-sed for a long time and a fishpond which he gives to the infirmary of the convent'. These are all the known records of the Abbey of Killenny. In 1228 Stephen de Lexington ordered that the old graves at Killenny Abbey, should be removed to Graigna-managh, but this was never done.

By 1227 this abbey had failed and had become so small and poor that it could not continue as an abbey. In that year 'B... Abbot of Froidmont, visiting the Irish Cistercian houses with full powers to reduce the poorer houses to be granges, to unite houses, to interdict, suspend and excommunicate all Gainsayers and even the monasteries themselves finding that the Abbey of Killenny is in debt, so that it can subsist no longer and that the monks are obliged to beg directs the transfer of Killenny with its property to Duiske ordering that the abbots and monks of the former house be well treated.'[4]

The procedure necessary for absorbing Killenny in Duiske was elaborate. First the Abbot of Froidmont, who came from France to visit the Irish Cistercian houses, directed the Union of the two abbeys, then his recommendation was confirmed by the Abbey of Clairvaux. Next the Abbots of Citeaux and the four elder daughters of Citeau viz La Ferte, Pontigny, Clairvaux and Morimund[5] added their final confirmation and lastly the Abbey of Duiske received a formal order on the subject: 'Confirmation by the Abbots of Citeaux La Ferte, Pontigny, Clairvaux and Morimund of the reduction of Killenny to a grange and its union with Duiske as directed by the Abbot of Froidmont ... ABBATIAM Vallis Dei iam in grangiam redactam...'.[6]

This grange acquired by Duiske was situated in the Middle Barrow Lowlands lying between the Castlecomer plateau on the west and the Leinster chain on the east. It is an area of drift-covered Carboniferous strata and Ordovician slates covered with limestone gravel which provides a soil containing lime almost everywhere. These soils vary greatly in depth from a thin rind to as much as 100 feet and

A carved stone from Killenny Abbey. Note the Mason's Mark +.

on the whole can be claimed as being exceptionally good. Jerpoint resisted the transfer to Duiske. The Celtic Abbey of Killenny had been a daughter house of Jerpoint and when both these houses became Cistercian, Jerpoint had a strong bond with Killenny. A dispute about this land broke out and lasted for one hundred and fifty years.

The union of Killenny as a grange of Duiske took place; in 1253[7] it was consented to by the Abbot of Mellifont, and in 1261 it was confirmed by the General Chapter.[8] This lasted until 1276 when the General Chapter decided to break up the union, and return Killenny to Jerpoint.[9] Duiske was furious about this and resisted, so much so that she was placed under interdict from 1276-78.[10] One can understand Duiske's anxiety and reaction. After all, the Old Abbey buildings had now been converted into grange buildings during the previous fifty years. In 1288 what is described as an amicable agreement was reached, namely that Duiske should take over the debts of Jerpoint to the amount of one thousand marks with a further undertaking to spend three hundred marks in addition on the lands of Jerpoint.[11] This was a vast financial undertaking by Duiske Abbey but she must have had the wherewithal to pay or else she would not have undertaken it.

In fact Duiske Abbey did fulfil this undertaking and agreed to do so. Charter 88 is an Inspeximus by P., Abbot of Dublin, H., Abbot of Mellifont and other Abbots of the order addressed to the Abbots of Citeaux, la Ferte, Pontigny, Clairvaux and Morimund, declaring that the Abbot of Jerpoint and his convent abandon all claims upon Killenny or upon the Grange of Annamult to the convent of Duiske for one thousand three hundred marks sterling money and bind themselves in one thousand marks accordingly. Consequently, in 1289 H., Abbot of Mellifont, J., Abbot of Fermoy, M., Abbot of Kil-

Killenny from the north east.

cooley and L., Abbot of Cashel sent a certificate to J., Abbot of Clairvaux saying that the transfer had been ratified, Duiske having paid Jerpoint one thousand marks and undertaken to pay three hundred and ten marks more within five years.[12] Jerpoint declared that without this money they would not meet their obligations.

Jerpoint certainly needed the money to pay off her debts. In Charter 88 there is an indenture between John, Abbot of Duiske, and Peter, Abbot of Jerpoint, giving the details of the payments made by Duiske on behalf of Jerpoint. Adam Blund of Callan was given one hundred and twenty marks, Walter Hay and other creditors of Thomastown were paid eighty marks, two Italian wool merchants were given forty marks, another called Leonard Teste was paid thirty marks, Robert Serman, burgess of New Ross, twenty marks, the Abbot of St Mary's Abbey, Dublin, twenty marks and Jerpoint was given sixty marks for redeeming their land and was further exonerated from wool merchant debts, namely five hundred and twenty marks due to Bendinus Pannyth, merchant of Lucca. And a further one hundred and twenty marks was allotted for eight sacks of wool and two hundred and ninety marks for the redemption of lands in the hands of Elias de Hipstone and Master Richard de Blancheville.[13]

48

The foregoing reveals a striking contrast between two neighbouring abbeys with regard to finance. In 1290 Thomas, Abbot of Jerpoint, was forced to execute a bond whereby he and his convent for £10,000 sterling would not disturb the convent of Duiske in their possession of Killenny or the grange of Annamult in consideration of which Duiske had paid one thousand three hundred marks.[14] However, it was not until 1362 when Abbot Philip of Jerpoint finally decided to give up his claim to the land that the dispute over Killenny and Annamult was settled. He agreed not to make further claims to these parcels and if he defaulted then he would pay £20,000 in silver to Duiske, £10,000 sterling to the Abbot of Citeaux, £1,000 in florins to the Pope for the Defence of The Holy Land, £5,000 sterling to the Earl of Gloucester and £1,000 in silver to the Earl of Ormonde.[15]

This is the end to a dispute which lasted for one hundred and fifty years. Despite this agreement arranged by the Abbot of Jerpoint and Duiske Abbey, they later decided that a further guarantee should be made. In 1424 Henry Fitz Henry O'Ryan confirmed the Charter of his ancestor to Duiske Abbey. Duiske, a Norman Abbey, decided that she should obtain the approval of the O'Ryans to this grant since the Killenny parcel that she had acquired was in O'Ryan territory and if she had the Irish chief's approval then she would not likely be dispossessed.[16]

The extent taken following the suppression of the house shows that the monastery then held land in counties Kilkenny, Carlow, Wexford and Cork. The lands in Carlow amounted to less than 100 acres and in Wexford to more than 2,000 acres, while the total possessions excluding the Cork lands amounted to more than 23,000 acres.

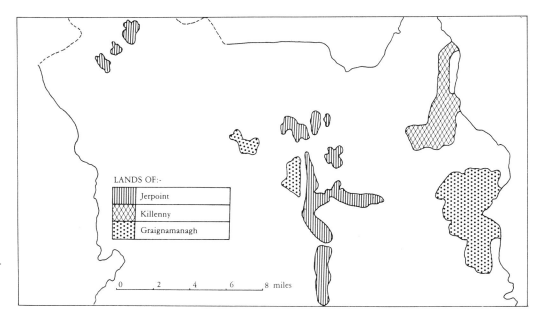

LANDS OF:-

Jerpoint

Killenny

Graignamanagh

0   2   4   6   8 miles

Map showing lands of Jerpoint, Graigna-managh and Killenny.

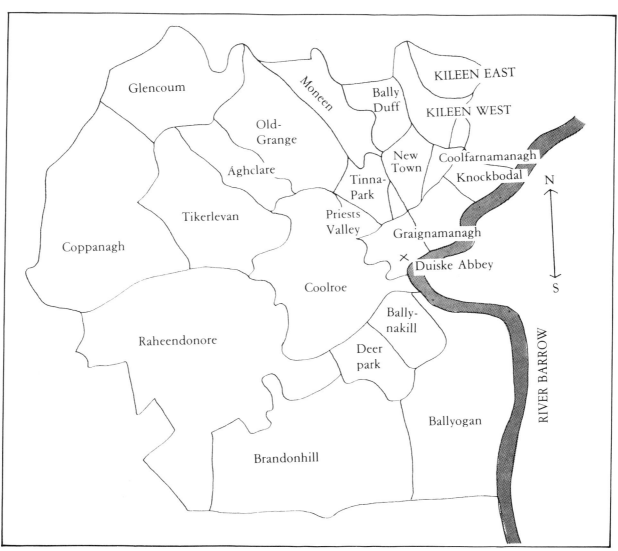

In the core of this large estate was Duiske Abbey and such a large bloc enabled the Cistercians to adhere to the directive that they should live 'far from the haunts of men.'

The home-farm lands of Duiske Abbey with the modern townland areas named.

DUISKE; GRAIGUENAMANAGH,
CO. KILKENNY f1204

Townland	AC.	R.	P.	6 inch Os. sheet	Townland	AC.	R.	P.	6 inch Os. sheet
				Kilkenny					
Aghlare				25	Duninga	4807	0	26	21
Ballyduff				25/29	Grange Lower				21/25
Ballynakill				29	Grange Upper				21/25
Ballyogan				29/33	Powerstown West	15	3	11	25
Brandonhill				29/33	Mount Loftus	48	0	23	25
Coolfarnamanagh				29	Killeen East	116	3	17	25/29
Coolieran				25	Killeen West	292	0	15	25/29
Coolroe				29	Annamult	1351	2	2	23/24/27/28
Coppanagh				25/29	Baunlusk				23
Deerpark				29	Grange Hill				20
Glencoum				25/29	Grange				23
Graiguenamanagh				29	Grange Cuffe				23
Knockbodaly				29	Kilmog (Racecourse)				23
Moneen				25/29	Raheenduff	1934	2	24	23
Newtown				29	Rossdama				18/19/22/23
Oldgrange	12422	3	10	25/29	Grange Wat.	77	0	0	Carlow 8
Priests Valley				29	Garraun Lower	450	2	18	19/23
Raheendonore				33	Garraun Upper	496	3	31	19/23
Tickerlevan				33	Grange Demesne	253	3	30	Wexford 18
Tinnapark				29	Grange Lower	444	0	2	18
Barrowmount				21/25	Grange Upper	496	3	31	18/24

Total	23209	0	0

Quality of Land

Good quality land was necessary for abbeys both in the early days of foundation and in their subsequent growth and expansion. In the early days which coincided with the recruitment of monks and lay brothers and the construction of buildings, light quality friable soils were an advantage. The ease of exploitation of land consequent on thriving recruitment, provided a surplus realised in capital for building projects and lasted to c. 1270. By that time the influence of the Mendicant Orders, chiefly the Franciscans, caused a loss in recruitment of lay brothers to the Cistercians. The Cistercian wore as an indication of its involvement in agricultural practice a black apron-like garment called the scapular, and this is still worn by Cistercians all over the world today. Agricultural progress among the Cistercians depended almost entirely on the lay brothers and with competition from the Mendicant Orders there was a gradual decline in their numbers, but the fortunes of the abbey did not decline, because during this period the wool trade with Western Europe was increasing. Sheep rearing demanded less labour than tillage, fewer lay brothers reduced the need for cultivated crops and land of good quality not needed for sheep rearing could easily be leased. About 1290 in fact the monks found the system of land leasing and money rents to be very profitable and this coincided with their great period of rebuilding. Good quality land could provide a range of products depending on whether the market was in favour of corn or sheep. In the early phase of sub-letting the intrinsic quality of good land was wealth to an Abbey.

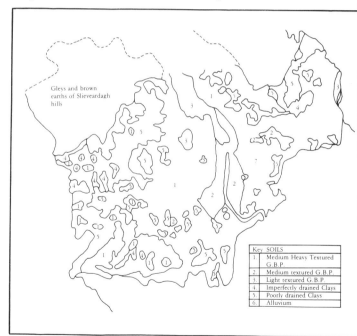

Key SOILS	
1	Medium Heavy Textured G.B.P.
2	Medium textured G.B.P.
3	Light textured G.B.P.
4	Imperfectly drained Clays
5	Poorly drained Clays
6	Alluvium

Map of soil types
Reproduced from map supplied by courtesy of
Bord Taluntais

The monks of Graignamanagh had 23,000 acres of land, but some attention must now be given to examining the quality and suitability of this land for agricultural enterprises. In general there are four main types of soil in Ireland, brown earths, grey brown podzols, gleys and peats. Map p. 51 shows the quality of the lands of Graignamanagh Abbey: sixteen thousand of her twenty three thousand acres were on the Blackstairs series of podzols and blanket peats. She was not as well off as Jerpoint who had nine thousand acres of excellent tillage land on what has recently been called 'Kilkenny's Golden Vein'.[1] Graignamanagh's only good endowment tillage area was in the Grange of Annamult where she had thirteen hundred acres and two thousand acres in Grange Cuff. Well indeed may Abbot Thomas of Graignamanagh have been pleased when the lands of the suppressed Abbey of Killenny were handed over to him, for in this way he received four thousand acres of excellent tillage land and it is not surprising that Jerpoint was reluctant to give this up. Activities as far as can be gleaned from the medieval documents of Graignamanagh Abbey were sheep rearing, milling and fishing.

Sheep Rearing

It is a commonplace to say that wool was the leading export of Medieval England and the commodity which determined much of the political as well as the economic activities of the Middle Ages. Its history as an article of commerce goes back a long way, but the earliest systematic accounts of its shipment abroad date only from Edward I's reign 1272-1307. Unfortunately documentation in Medieval Ireland for the same period is scarce and such evidence as can be obtained in the Memoranda Rolls is in the form of debts to foreign wool merchants. In England, Boston in Lincolnshire was the principal port for the export of wool and in its hinterland were situated the many monasteries that were supplying Italian merchants at this time. In Ireland the monasteries were also supplying Italian merchants; on the domestic front it was convenient and profitable for them to do so due to the problem of the reduction in numbers of lay brothers. Fewer men were required in this industry and the sale of wool provided them with a source of income for the erection and repair of their buildings.

Different breeds of sheep produce different grades of whool and the same breed of sheep will produce wool varying very much in quality according to the type of soil and the nature of the pasture on which it is raised. According to the soil suitability tests, the soils of the granitic terrain of Graignamanagh were deficient in cobalt and would present problems in the lambing season. Irish monasteries were involved in sheep rearing mainly for wool. For their domestic needs, they required a placement of one third of their clothing annually as that was the amount that had to be discarded and given to the poor. They also sold wool to the Italian merchants by the practice of Forward Sales. However if a bad winter came, such as occurred in 1281-2 and again in 1296-7, or a severe spring, as in 1281, a great number of sheep and lambs might be lost and the abbey would be unable to fulfill its contract. This happened frequently, for the fortunes of the wool trade can be traced in the list of debts incurred by the monks. It would assist in comparing the data from the various sources, if a rough equation could be devised between the number of sheep owned, the number of sacks of wool produce and the profits made. Robert of Grosseteste calculates that 1,000 sheep on a good pasture should give fifty marks, a year's income, while from other sources it would appear that an average yield was equivalent to four or five sacks per thousand sheep. Heavy debts on the part of the monasteries became common in the last quarter of the thirteenth century when the monasteries were involved in building projects. In 1299 Graignamanagh Abbey owed to the Ricardi £466-66 of which £66.66 was to be paid on demand and the rest at the rate of £100 in wool per year.[3] This was the produce of 2,000 sheep over a span of six years, on average 350 sheep per year. Further demands were made on the sheep farming activities of Duiske. In 1300 Edward I was at war with Scotland and needed money for this. He sent letters of credence to many ecclesiastical houses in Ireland and one of these was Duiske.[4] The King was anxious for money and agreed to remit to Crown 'debtors' two-thirds of their debts, provided that for the remaining one third they came with horses and arms to Scotland for the war, and that the same be expended in wages etc according to the number of men brought and the time they stayed in the King's service and 'whereas the convent of Duiske owes the firm of the Ricardi of Lucca £342-17-3 to be paid within four years, as of record in the Exchequer Rolls and the Ricardi are bound to the King in a large amount, it is ordered: THAT in consideration of £114-5-9 now paid by the convent to John Deneger for the wages of six men-at arms and horses twelve hobelarii, and sixty-two footmen for the war above the whole of their debt to the aforesaid merchants shall be extinguished.'[5] In other words the King was glad of the ready cash. This was one of the drawbacks of being a landowner in Medieval Ireland, for the Cistercian houses like other religious houses had to supply soldiers for the King's service and the Abbot of Duiske, like other religious, had to collect this from his tenants.

The Mills of Duiske

The Cistercians of Duiske were obviously exploiting the granges for tillage and the slopes of Brandon Mountain for sheep-rearing. Because of this they had corn mills and fulling mills (tuck). The extent

Records show that amongst the items supplied by the tenants of Duiske Abbey was beer brewed by them. Hops are used in flavouring beer. This carving may be an attempt to carve a hop.

54

of these enterprises is shown by the number of mills they owned. On the Duiske River near the Abbey, they had three mills, one at Ballymills, one of the site later occupied by Cushen Brothers's Mill and then the Abbey Mills.[6] They also had water mills on their granges, one at Old Abbey,[7] one on the Grange of Downying[8] and another in Grange Wate.[9] As on the Duiske River, a mill race had to be cut at Killenny to provide a steep gradient for water power. There is an interesting lease of a mill for five years, that was agreed at Tulachany in 1440. Philip the Abbot of Duiske leased to Thomas White twenty acres of land in Annamult from Freusdyche to Merdyche between the Abbey lands and the lands of Dunfert and from Adameslaede to Kylmochone, with half the profits of the mill and the river:'the said Thomas to bear half the cost of repairing the mill and the whole cost of repairing the road thereto, and to pay twelve pence annually towards the repair of the monastery; the monastic tithes to be paid as before.'[10] Judging by the terms of this lease, mills in Medieval Duiske were a profitable possession. Furthermore, these mills reflect the economy of the monastic estate either for wool or corn.

A section of the 'right of way' leading to Clohastia Castle and the weir.

Part of the Stile 'built triangularwise' at entrance to 'right of way' looking north east.

Fisheries

Fisheries were a very important possession of the Cistercians. Due to monastic observance and to the fact that the Rule of St Bernard required them to dispense charity in the abbey guest houses, they required vast quantities of fish. The main type of fish caught in the River Barrow and the River Nore was eels. For this purpose eel weirs were erected. On the River Barrow in the vicinity of the Abbey, they had three eel weirs,[11] on the grange of Old Abbey, Killenny, one eel weir[12] and on the grange of Annamult half an eel weir.[13] This 'half an eel weir' sounds peculiar but the monks of the grange of Annamult had rights to only one bank of the Nore and the Cistercians of Jerpoint owned the other bank — hence 'half an eel weir'.

The monks welcomed gifts of fishing weirs and some gifts are recorded in the charters. In Charter 80 of the Abbey of Duiske there is a grant by Henry Fitz Henry Roche for the benefit of his soul and that of Olive his wife etc to the convent of Duiske of rights to fish in the River Barrow from Poulmuntath to Portgrenan. Polmuntath is the modern Polmounty on the River Barrow and Portgrenan is Thomastown on the River Nore.[14] In Charter 42 there is a grant by Nicholas le Marchis, for the good of his soul etc to the convent of Duiske, of the fish pond called Cordredan with its liberties etc to hold free of rent for ever.[15] Coraidh means a fishing weir and the fish pond of Chory O'Dradan or Cordredan was apparently a pool of the River Barrow, located somewhere between Borris and Leighlinbridge. Eel weirs consist of an obstruction across a river with a net called a coghill net placed across a gap in the weir. In the autumn the eels migrate downstream and it is during their downstream journey that a large number swim into the net. Today the use of the 'Coghill' is illegal; nevertheless, this one-time practice survives in the Graig-

namanagh district as 'Cudyale' and there are families in the area who have inherited the skill. The nets are placed across the gaps in the weirs and people who carry on 'Cudyaling' have the admiration and sympathy of the local people as this was an activity reserved for the ascendancy class in post monastic days. One of the Abbey eel weirs is still visible underwater just below Molsha's Rock, (i.e. St Lazerian's Rock) one hundred yards above the Abbey Wood (Graig Wood) and another is visible at low tide fifty yards above Poulnasillog, Ballyogan eels were used for fish stew whilst young eels were made into elver cheese.

Polmounty on the River Barrow. The monks of Duiske Abbey were granted fishing rights here.

The Abbey and the Community

The Cistercians were primarily agriculturalists, hence the Acorn Stone found in Duiske Abbey. The word 'acorn' originally meant 'fruit of the field', allied to the word 'acre'.

It has already been mentioned in Chapter 7 that Duiske Abbey took over the debts of Jerpoint Abbey and it is fitting that an explanation should be given as to how the monks managed their estates. In order to gain maximum control, efficiency and progress a very thorough system of book-keeping, formulated in Citeau for the management of granges, was used. Their management system was a masterpiece of thoroughness and secured the successful establishment of their lands.

The foundation Charter of Duiske mentions the monks, 'their men and their tenants', who lived on their monastic estates. These people paid the monks not in money but in food, kind or services. This was a custom to which they held tenaciously right down to the dissolution of the Abbey.

The amount of work required of each tenant was prescribed as follows:- [1]

District	Cottager	Plough days	Cart-days	Boon-days	Weeding days
Duiske	22	12	12	12	12
Raheendonore	14	12	12	17	17
Tullaghanny	12	8	8	16	16
Grange of William Carraghe	11	4	4	12	12
Tikerleven		3	3	6	6
Killeen	4	3	3	4	4
Garvok		2	2	2	2

The number of boon days or days spent harvesting the crop was similar to the number of days required for weeding and the number of cart days was similar to the number of plough days.

The roll on which the number of days worked was kept was called the Rotulorum and the person in charge of it was called the Custos of the Rotulorum. He kept a roll of the names of his tenants and for each a tally stick. He had to hear statements from the infirmarian, the guestmaster, the stewards, the cellarers, the keepers of the minor granges in the presence of the Procurator. The Keeper of the tally sticks and rolls was also required to convene a meeting with the sub cellarer, the infirmarian, the porter, the monk baker, and the custos of the grange for this aspect of administration. The meetings were usually held on Mondays but if a solemn feast-day occurred then it would be delayed until Tuesday. This was regarded as a very important meeting: if any monk was not present at the auditing, then he had to mention this at the next Chapter meeting, and for his neglect he would have had to go without his pittance for that day.

To all these work days were added certain payments in victuals and animals. In Raheendonore, the fourteen tenants had to supply seventeen hens, twelve cakes of bread, twelve gallons of beer, twelve candles and one pig and one sheep from each flock numbering seven or more.[2] On the demesne land of Duiske, twenty-two cottagers gave twelve hens, twelve cakes, a quarter of beef at Christmas, one sheep from each flock numbering seven or more and from every brewing of beer one gallon of the better beer.[3] The tenants of Tikerlevan supplied six hens,[4] the four cottagers of Killeen four hens,[5] those of Garvok two hens,[6] the eleven cottagers of the Grange of William Carraghe twelve hens,[7] the twelve cottagers of the Grange of Tullaghanny sixteen hens, in all a total of some fifty-nine hens was given to the monks.

The relationship that developed between the tenants of the lands of Duiske Abbey and the monks encouraged the people to keep accounts, to make calculations, to measure accurately, to watch the market and to check their accounts. They drew their attention to costs, yields of seed and the variations between them and they also introduced the people to the idea of number, value and profit. Thus the tenants knew what the expected yield for crops was. Barley gave eight times the quantity sown, rye seven times, beans six times, peas six times, wheat and rye six times and oats four times.

The people who lived on the monastic lands usually had a monk to look after their spiritual needs. A person so appointed was called a Rector and such a person as the Rector of Duiske officiated for the seculars in Duiske Abbey; similarly the Rector of Annamult, the Rector of Tullaghanny, the Rector of Ballyle, the Rector of Kylcombre, the Rector of Kylcromylassey.[8] The traditional way of paying this person was to pay him a tithe, that is a tenth of the produce of land in the parish he served, thus he received the tenth sheaf, the tenth piglet and so on. From the tithes collected we can ascertain the unit of measurement and the nature of the products that a grange was producing, since they were collected annually. The sheaves, called 'garb', were tied in couples termed 'copp' on most granges, every tenth couple being given to pay the priest. Tenants in Tikerleven[9] gave half a copp. Such sheaves would have provided valuable material for thatching. Sometimes the grain was threshed, wheat and oats being contributed instead. The seed was calculated in gallons and was known as a measure. Not all measures on Cistercian estates in Ireland were the same. On the lands of St Mary's Abbey, Dublin St Glennokes'[10] measure of 1 peck equal to 9 gallons was used; in Dobbere[11] a grange of the same abbey, a peck of 12 gallons was used; on the grange of Dunbrody[12] a peck was 16 gallons and in all cases a copp or couple was 10 measures.

Duiske Abbey had a different unit of measurement known as Kilkenny measure. This was a peck containing 24 gallons.[13] On Duninga the Rector received as customs 40 pecks of corn and oats,[14] the Rector of Duiske received 7 pecks of corn and oats,[15] the Rector of Annamult[16] received 30 pecks

58

of corn and 30 pecks of oats, the Rector of Tullachany 30 pecks,[17] whilst as customs to the monastery, the people of Wood Grange gave 20 measures of corn and 20 of oats[18] and for tithes 10 pecks of corn and 10 pecks of oats,[19] and those in the Grange of William Carraghe and Grange of Dorringa 40 pecks of corn and 40 pecks of oats.[20]

The price of a copp was the same at Dunbrody, Dublin, Duiske, Mellifont, and Bective. For Mellifont mention is made of 4 copps 53s.4d.,[21] Bective (Balroy) 13s.4d.[22] St Mary's Abbey, Dublin (Daveston) 4 copp 53s.4d., 13s.4d.[23] and Duiske Abbey ½ copp 6s.8d. (Tikerleven).[24]

Such involvement introduced the local people to lessons in good management by responsible men and necessitated the keeping of account rolls by a bursar on the grange. The Cistercian system of audit and accounts spread to Ireland from Citeaux. A monk on the Grange of Farringdon belonging to Beaulieu Abbey, Hampshire, wrote down the rules for the management of granges. This was an abbey which was founded directly from Citeaux and its arrangements were doubtless a replica of those used at the Mother House c. 1220. From the formula used in the extants of Duiske Abbey it is possible to see the same type of auditing. In all there are twelve rules for this and these give a wonderful impression of efficiency and thoroughness. Rule one deals with the time when the auditing should take place, that is on the Feast of St Michael, 29 September; 'We are accustomed to make an assessment of the granges and workshops of our Abbey by using tally rods and count rolls.' Thus it is easy to explain how the lay-brother managed to have all the information available by relying on notches cut out of sticks or barn posts i, ii, iii, iv. Each grange had its own account at the abbey. At the weekly audit when a monk had his audit ready, another monk would compute this in the camera. (The camera of the Abbot was the Abbot's quarters.) The same monk had to show these accounts to the Abbot four times a year, namely Christmas Day, Easter Sunday, the Nativity of St John the Baptist and the Feast of St. Michael. This idea of quarterly accounts gave the monastery a good idea as to how the economy of a grange was progressing and decisions relating to improvement could be taken. Finally there was the annual audit at the grange, submitted at the annual audit of the abbey itself.

Goods that had been sold but awaiting the settlement of the bill by a customer were called *arreragium* and this was allowed in respect of one year only. Money paid into the Abbey Exchequer without any having been withdrawn was called a *liberatio*. If money repayments were made to the Central Fund this was called a Ramento. The only officials who could make repayments and make a *liberatio* at the same time due to the nature of their work were the cobblers and the smiths. Each annual statement had the previous year's surplus written on top of the account. Goods obtained by one workshop from another were to be exchanged at cost price whilst goods sold to outsiders were sold at a competitive price, but the profit had to be stated and written down.

If the manager of a grange wanted to buy property, he could pay for this out of that grange's own contribution to the central fund, if it had enough deposited there. If it had not enough contributions, then he could on behalf of that grange borrow from the central fund and pay back later. If it did borrow from its own reserve then it had to pay this back later as well. Within this system the tenants of Duiske Abbey were secure and permanent and organised and each successive generation of tenants must have learned and benefited greatly from their contact with the monks and their splendid example of estate management.

The Abbey Treasury

British Library, British Museum. 'Sancti Salvatore in Hibernia'.

In the previous section of this chapter, we saw how the monks taught the people number, value, measurement and an auditing system based mainly on agricultural enterprises. They were equally attentive and painstaking with the care of the title deeds of their possessions. It was a monk called Brother Michael of Stanley Abbey, the Mother House of Duiske Abbey, who described this method and wrote it down in Latin. This has been translated as follows: 'Here begins the titles of the Charters. Firstly of the charters pertaining to places whose names begin with A, taken with B and so on. In this arrangement of titles this method is carried out viz; immediately after the title of each charter are placed the confirmations if any of that charter, after these confirmations are placed other deeds, appertaining to the same and it is to be noted that the number which is written at the head of the titles indicates in what place the separate deeds are deposited. But the dot represents in what order they are. The small circles show which are the charters placed in the broad chest.' [1]

Fortunately a medieval list which gives only a brief summary of the contents of documents belonging to Stanley Abbey is held in the British Museum. This is in manuscript form, a thin long folio of seventeen pages written in a thirteenth century hand. It is described in the folio catalogue thus:- 'Liber membranaceus in folio, in quo habentur Tituli Privilegorum et Indulgentiarum finales Coricordiae et tituli Cartarum ad varia loca pektinentium folia membranacea.' In this collection there are four charters of Duiske Abbey the details of which are as follows:-

Alphabetical Order	Placed Broad Chest	Dots in what Order	Place in which Deposited	
Sancti Salvatoris	O	· ·	XIX	H. Ossiriensis Episcopi de protectione Domus. Et de Duabus Capellis.
Sancti Salvatoris				Comitis Willemi Marescalli de confirmatione terrarum etc aliorum quae antecessores sui eidem Domici contulerunt.
				Hed carta est in quadam cass* (sive lata archa) ij de adjunctione Abbatie frigidi montis; quae est in quadam piscide*

The place in the treasury or muniments room where the charters were shelved must have been numbered in alphabetical order. 'XIX' corresponds to the nineteenth letter of the alphabet 'S', hence 'sancti Salvatoris in Hibernia'. The small dots arranged . : would suggest that the episcopal Deed was placed by itself, with nothing under or on top of it whilst the : suggests that William Marshal's charter was deposited on top of Cartae ij. With such a methodical arrangement of cataloguing and storing, it is easy to see how charters were readily available when required for renewal or confirmation. The Index List compiled in conjunction with the deeds in the muniments room left plenty of space between each alphabet section to allow for new entries to be made as and when the monks received additional gifts of land or churches or privileges or indulgences or whatever. It is not unreasonable to presume that those monks who came from Stanley to Duiske adopted the Cistercian method of organisation in this abbey too.

The Fair

The fair for Graignamanagh was held not in the vicinity of the abbey but on the opposite bank of the River Barrow at Tinnahinch. It was held on 29 September, the Feast of St Michael. There were certain privileges relating to Fairs such as pontage, lastage, stallage, intangthef, Wayf and Stray. Pontage was a toll paid for crossing the River Barrow to come to the fair, the wooden ford in those days being in the vicinity of the present Butler Castle, which was not built until the sixteenth century. Lastage was a fee paid by hawkers to allow them to carry goods through a fair and stallage was the fees charged for erecting stalls at the fair. Intangthef was the privilege whereby the court in Duiske could call to judgement anyone caught thieving at the fair. Wayf applied to two classes of goods namely those

which were found whose owner was unknown and secondly goods taken by a thief and thrown away by him while being pursued to prevent being apprehended, and finally stray, which meant any chattel or beast which had no owner or any domestic animal that had left its enclosure or proper place and was wandering at large or was lost.

Such regulations show the beginnings of commercial trading. It is unlikely that the profits of this fair went to the monks, but belonged to the Corporate town of Newtown (the Nova Villa). However it was a great advantage for the monks to have it close by. The Cistercian laws held that if a fair necessitated an overnight stay away from the abbey, then the monks had to employ a secular to do their factoring for them. Some fairs like the Lammas Fair in Ballycastle had their special line of goods such as the confectionery known as Yellow Man; in Tinnahinch it was mutton pasties. This was known as the Mir (a portion) Michael, Michael's portion. Agneis, the wife of King Laeghaire Mac Niall 'took on herself' an obligation to bestow a sheep out of every flock she owned, and a portion of each meal to the poor — hence the Michaelmas sheep and Mír Michael. In the tenth century this custom was revived by King Doncadh of Ossory. He ordered that three leather wallets should be kept in each house. In one of these bags the tithes of the meals were kept, in another the mutton and in the third herbs to garnish the meat. This was then distributed amongst the poor. From this practice grew the custom of eating mutton pasties on the 29 September at the Fairs of Duiske.[1]

In 1541 when the Abbey was dissolved and the lands were transferred to the Crown, the King gave a lease of the estate to J. Butler and this became the manor of Duiske. The manor fairs were then held on the waste ground of the former abbey quarry site now known as the Fair Green.

Times of Change

It has already been indicated that the forerunner of Cistercian monasticism in Ireland was Celtic monasticism with perhaps some Celtic-Benedictine in a few houses. Less than one hundred years after the foundation of Mellifont, there was a tendency to revert to the Celtic spirit. Furthermore the Norman Invasion had taken place and a political dimension was now influencing the monastic households. The trouble in Irish houses was first reported to the General Chapter in 1216 when the official Visitor of the Order was refused entry to carry out his annual inspection of the house.[1] The same thing happened at Jerpoint, and the Abbots of Baltinglass, Killenny, Kilbeggan and Bective supported her.[2] The General Chapter deposed the Abbot of Mellifont and Jerpoint immediately and the other four abbots were disciplined.

The matter regarding Mellifont came before the General Chapter in 1221, the story of the collapse of monastic discipline, the lack of care of monastic buildings and properties, conspiracies in the monasteries and the lack of success in achieving correction.[3] In 1226 the problem was still not resolved and the problem of Mellifont came before the General Chapter once more.

In 1227 another visitation of Mellifont was conducted by Bernard, Abbot of Froidmont and the Abbot of Buildwas in Shropshire.[4] By now the trouble and opposition had spread to other daughter houses of Mellifont, namely Assaroe, Boyle, Fermoy, Abbeydorney and Newry. The foreign visitors thought that this had been promoted by the mother house Mellifont who influenced these daughter houses during her abbot's annual visitation of them, so word was easily passed around. The French Abbot of Froidmont and the Abbot of Buildwas considered that this problem could be resolved if the Abbot of Mellifont was removed and that her daughter houses should be taken from her and fostered by other houses. In this way the conspiracy and power bloc would be broken. The General Chapter agreed, Maigue was fostered by Margam,[6] Baltinglass by Fountains,[7] Inishlounaght by Furness[8] and Killenny was too small, and could be reduced to a grange and given to Graignamanagh.[9] All this was reported to the General Chapter and the following year they asked the Abbot of Clairvaux to continue with the work of reform. In 1228 the Abbot of Clairvaux chose the Abbot of Stanley in Wiltshire to assist him. This was Stephen de Lexington, destined to become one of the leading men of the Order,[10] becoming Abbot of Savigny in 1229[11] and of Clairvaux itself in 1243.[12] It was only natural that Abbot Stephen of Stanley should carry out his legislation from Graignamanagh as he had to make an annual visitation to this his daughter house anyway. Stephen brought the Abbot of Buildwas and the Abbot of Margam with him, carried out his visitation of the Irish houses and then reported back to the General

Chapter. He reported the failure of the previous years' visitation: the new Abbots of Jerpoint and Mellifont were opposed by their communities, the Baltinglass community rejected their new foster mother Fountains, English monks were ejected by the Irish monks of Maigue. Everything of the Cistercian Order was gone except the wearing of the habit, he declared.[13]

Stephen held a meeting in Duiske in 1228.[14] After all, Duiske did not belong to the Mellifont bloc and her discipline was assured by the Abbey of Stanley. However the reduction of Killenny to a grange and its donation to Duiske brought her into dispute with Jerpoint, as explained in Chapter 7. Stephen held two meetings of Abbots, one in Duiske and one in Dublin explaining to them the problems of the Irish houses.[15] He must have established sufficient liaison with those houses represented at Duiske, for on 27 July he went to Mellifont where he was freely admitted and in which he spent seven days. The replacement Abbot of Mellifont offered to resign, in order to promote Stephen's work of reconciliation.[16] Stephen was reluctant to accept but knowing that he had a good candidate in Jocelyn, Prior of Beaubec in France, he decided to do so.[17] Stephen decided that forty Mellifont monks should be sent to Continental monasteries and that they could not be re-admitted to an Irish house without permission from the Abbot of Clairvaux.[18] He allowed twelve monks and sixteen brothers to remain in Mellifont.[19] Since the new Abbot was a Frenchman, he decided that it would be futile to admit a man as a monk who did not know French or Latin.[20] The intrusion of the Frenchman into the head mother house of Mellifont would improve relations with Clairvaux and the General Chapter and promote the Cistercian way of life, he thought.

All was not well yet however. Trouble arose when the visitors went to Maigue. The visitors were the Abbot of Abington and the Cantor of Graignamanagh [21] but they were not admitted; the Abbey was fortified against them. The latter visitors had to appeal to the Norman bishop of Limerick, Hugh de Burgh, who advised a forced entry of the monastery.[22] When this was achieved, the Bishop turned the monks of Maigue over to the Cistercians, whose abbot was then deposed and a new one elected.

Stephen called a chapter in June, in Dublin. Fourteen abbots attended, half of them from Anglo-Norman houses, and the other half the new foreign appointments of the Visitor General.[23] Stephen drew up a thirteen point plan and put the Abbot of Dublin and the Abbot of Graignamanagh in charge of seeing that it was put into action. These thirteen points are now quoted in full from *The Church and The Two Nations in Medieval Ireland* by J. A. Watt and give an idea as to what was at fault and in need of correction, in Irish Cistercian monasteries.[24]

1. No one shall be admitted to be a monk, no matter what his nationality, unless he can confess his faults in French or Latin, in order that when the visitors and correctors of the order come he can understand them and be understood by them.
2. The charters and all legal documents of houses shall be kept together in such safe keeping as shall make it impossible in the future for wicked men to steal them or use them for fraudulent purposes.
3. The rule shall in future be explained only in French and the monks' chapter conducted in either French or Latin so that in future anyone who wishes to be received as a monk must have attended such a school as would teach him to conduct himself less uncouthly.

4. As punishment for the conspiracies which have arisen generally in Irish houses, it is strictly forbidden for any monk of that people to be appointed Abbot, in order that obedience to the order be fully proved and that having first learned how to be pupils, they may in due time and place be the more capable masters.

5. It is forbidden under pain of anathema for any lands or holdings to be alienated without the prior consent and confirmation of the father Abbot. This is commanded under pain of deposition from office and removal from the council.

6. No property shall be leased for a longer period than seven years so that there shall be a recent memory of the transaction. It is forbidden to execute a lease without the appropriate safeguards of previously seeking serious and responsible advice and with appropriate consultation taken publicly and formally.

7. So that for the future the property of houses should not be wasted nor the crime of simony committed through lack of forethought, it is strictly commanded under the penalties already mentioned that monks in the future should not buy land or accept patronage of Churches unless correct and careful inquisition has first been made, so that any entry or possession shall be fully legal and secure in title.

8. All officials of monasteries and granges who have responsibility for possessions, are strictly commanded to render true and accurate account to their abbot and council or to those specially appointed for the purpose by the abbot. Whatever is kept back will be held against the concealer, for theft or holding property and he will be liable to the established penalties for these crimes.

9. It is commanded under the same penalty that no brother shall sell anything without the consent or licence of his abbot or cellarer.

10. Monks and brothers who have been dismissed to other houses shall not be recalled without the special permission of the Abbot of Clairvaux, properly obtained without falsehood or suppression of the truth, a grace or dispensation obtained by lying or concealing the truth is ipso iure invalid.

11. On pain of anathema, deposition from office, removal from the council, it is strictly forbidden that ever for the future should any woman be received as a nun in the houses of Ireland, because of the shameful disorderliness and scandals to which this practice has given rise.

12. By authority of the order and of the General Chapter the Abbots of Dublin and Graignamanagh are strictly commanded on their obedience to promulgate the above instructions, in their exact form, their seals attached, in all the houses in Ireland.

13. Every house shall keep carefully its own copy of these instructions. The said abbots shall order them to be read once a month for a year, under pain of serious and certain sentence.

It is not the intention of this book to explore how these thirteen points affected the remaining thirty-two Abbeys in Ireland. It is relevant however that they can be studied in as far as they affected the Abbey of Graignamanagh itself. On the whole there are very few cases of litigation recorded in the Justiciary Rolls, no case of an Abbot being deposed for misrule or despoiling of property in the Papal Registers and very few civil cases. Nevertheless the question of the ownership of the Killenny Grange arose again in 1252[25] and we find that Abbot Thomas the second produced the charter relating to this for inspection, and that it was granted to Duiske in perpetual alms. The inspection of his charter was witnessed by William, Bishop of Bath and Wells, Godfrey de Lezignan, the King's brother Ralph Fitz Nicholas, John Maunsell, Provost of Beverley, Master William of Kilkenny, the Archdeacon of Coventry, Robert de Muscegros, Robert Walerand, Nicholas de St Maur, Henry le Plytevin, Roger de Lokinton, Nobert le Noreis and on the following day the King confirmed this charter, as did William the Marshal followed by the same signatories. The availability of this charter was in accord with point two of Stephen's Thirteen point plan. On the same day the Abbot Thomas II gave three gold marks to the King for the inspection and confirmation of this.[26]

In the Civil Court of 15th February 1311 the Jurors found that Maurice, Thomas and John Macmurghut robbed the Abbot of Duiske at New Grange of twenty-seven cows and that brother Gilbert the Granger received from Maurice thirteen of the cows without licences of the King's Court and that he also received from William Fyn two heifers which the latter stole from the Abbot's Wodegraunge. The Judge allowed restitution to be made so Gilbert the grangemaster was not found guilty.[27]

Under Cistercian regulations he would have been breaking Point 8 of Stephen's plan. However in 1306 there is a peculiar lease of land. John de Fresingfeud (Freshford) acknowledges in writing, that the Abbot of Dowysky demised to him the grange called Batesgraunge in Fothard for twenty years from Michaelmas. Provided that John may hold the grange for his life, the abbot may enter and hold it to him and his successors after the twenty years would be completed. Besides this he will acquit the abbot against the Bishop of Meath and the Dean of St Patrick's Dublin, collectors of the Papal Tenth, of seventy marks for the issues of the granges for the said twenty years.[28] This was in contradiction of Point 6 which only allowed a lease of land for seven years; however the fact that John de Fresingfeud acknowledged this transaction 'in writing' may have satisfied the requirements.

Abbot Stephen de Lexington wanted all gifts to be properly ascertained, so that no confusion might arise at a later date. An example as to how churches should be acquired as mentioned in Point 7 is seen in Charter forty, when Duiske acquired Tulachany and Tikerlevan he himself being a signatory to the agreement.[29]

It was not the custom for Cistercian Abbeys nor was it allowed by the Order to have nuns in monasteries. The practice however was not unknown in Ireland. Some double monasteries existed in the Houses of the Canons Regular of St Augustine and it would appear that there were nuns in Mellifont Abbey,[30] and Jerpoint.[31] Abbot Stephen ordered their removal. Besides, it was not until 1252 that the Cistercian General Chapter instituted the Order of Cistercian Nuns. There is no direct complaint made about Duiske Abbey, but the question arises as to what was meant by 'Teampal Na Mna'. Here attention is drawn to the word 'Na Mna' rather than 'na mban'. Therefore this was either a Lady Chapel (dedicated to Our Lady) or a church given by some female benefactor. However the practice of the Normans having Lady Chapels may infer a Church dedicated to Our Lady.

The Monks' Code

Duiske Abbey is one of the most fortunate abbeys in Ireland, in that a book written by the Abbot Visitor is still extant. This is known as 'Stephen de Lexington's Letter Book'. It is not a book in the sense that it is a cohesive work. Furthermore, Stephen de Lexington never thought that seven hundred and seventy-seven years later it would be published to allow us to have an idea of what was happening in the Abbey. During the Visitation, the visitor interviews each man, both monk and lay-brother living in the Abbey and on the Granges. He then writes down comments on these interviews and clarifies and corrects any point that might arise during an interview. At the end of the Visitation, he would summarise his findings and read them to the community. During the Visitation of 1228 Abbot Stephen wrote out ninety-six points which would appear to have risen during the interviews. The points are not structured in the sense that comments on the infirmary are dealt with together, nor comments on the Granges together, nor comments on the monks' diet, but single scattered comments referring to the life in the Abbey. Furthermore as with all Medieval Religion, reference is made to the Office and no person is named — hence the Prior, the Porter, the Wardrobe Keeper, the Master of the Lay-brothers. However it is necessary to state from the outset that this must be seen against the social background of Medieval days and many of the practices of those times no longer hold

in present day Cistercian Abbeys. I propose therefore to recall these practices and to explain them against the socio-cultural and economic background of those times.

Abbot Stephen directed that churches and chapels belonging to Master P should not be given to anyone except honest persevering chaplins, that each should have its own priest in residence, with the exception of the church of Annanult which he declared was very poor. The other churches and chapels referred to were Tulachany, Tikerlevan and Grange Castri.

'Master P' may be Master P of Christ Church who was entitled to the next presentation.[1] All officials of the monasteries, both monks and lay-brothers, were required to give clear and accurate accounts to the Abbot and Council of the house and were advised to keep written accounts for this purpose. If the Official concealed anything, this would be considered as stealing or possession of wealth and would therefore be in conflict with their vow of poverty and for this they would be punished. Lay-brothers could not sell anything of their own accord without permission of the Abbot or the cellarer. The punishment for the theft or the possession of wealth stated that he would get bread and water every Friday for a year, more coarse bread than was usual for forty days and a flogging at every Chapter for forty days. He would always be the last man in the procession. If he were a lay-brother his food would be left on the ground for forty days and he would have to stay sitting in the cloister without speaking except to the Abbot or his representative or in confession. He had to be present at all the Canonical Times and be whipped at each Chapter at which he was present for a year. The Abbot had power to add to these punishments if he desired. Here we must pause and scrutinise these directions. One must recall that in the Medieval period, the beverage was beer, every monastery had its brew house, tea and coffee were not known. Bread was the staple diet. The only substitute for beer was water. Regarding whipping as a punishment, in Medieval times this was not as bad as the secular practice of cutting off a man's hand, and sitting alone in the Cloister as a punishment was less severe than the secular practice of sitting in stocks in public and being spat upon. Furthermore I have not found any reference to indicate that any of these punishment methods were used.

The rule of enclosure was to be adhered to, permission was not to be given to the monks to go beyond the boundaries of the monastery to gossip, as this would encourage conspiracy and disorderliness; if a monk did, he would be punished for three days and on one of these he would be on bread and water. The Cistercians were vegetarians and Stephen directed that if anyone ate meat then he would be put on bread and water the next day. Nobody was to have meat unless he had ill-health. Stephen then directed that all the relatives of the monks and lay-brothers should be moved from the monastery and granges and it was the duty of the Prior, the Cellarer, and the Master of the lay-brothers to see to this, otherwise they would be on bread and water every Friday and should get a whipping in the Chapter. The monks were commanded not to buy lands or accept churches unless they verified beforehand through careful enquiries that they could have

free entry and safe possession of them. Lay-brothers were not allowed to accept food or drink in the houses of the local people within a distance of two leagues from the monastery without a bishop or an abbot being present. Anyone who exceeded this rule was put on bread and water for three days and got a whipping in the Chapter. Each time a monk or brother got drunk he was whipped in the Chapter and was put on bread and water. No woman was allowed to spend the night at the monastery gate (guest house) because it was against God's will and the Rule of the Order. If one did, then the Prior, the Cellarer, the Porter, or the Deputy Prior (if the Prior were absent) should receive a whipping in Chapter and be lightly punished for three days, one of the days being on bread and water. No piece of land was to be leased to a knight or powerful man. Meat was not to be served to a lay person either in his room or inside the enclosure, except to the Earl Marshal (founder of the Abbey) through sheer respect. The horses of 'Master P' were not to be allowed into the monastery quarters nor into any of the granges. If this were to happen then the Prior and the Cellarer were to be punished.

Stephen advocated that at least two suitable lay people should be appointed to take care of the groves and the fences of the monastery lands and the trees that were standing were not to be cut down for firewood, while there were so many lying on the ground. Anybody who broke this rule would be scolded in Chapter and be given a very heavy punishment.

Stephen advocated that the house in which there was a wine press should be separated from the infirmary yard by a high strong fence and that the servants' back door and the gate nearest to the infirmary should be closed up before the Feast of Saint Dionisius (Saint Denis). Abbot Stephen was very sensitive to the suppressed Abbey of Killenny, which had been reduced to a grange, and he commanded that no monk should stay outside on the granges or in Killenny for any reason whatsoever. Mass on the granges had to be celebrated there by a chaplain appointed especially to each grange. During their novitiate, the novices were to be free at a suitable time each day to study the Book of Usages and the liturgy of the Church. No monk or lay-brother who was being dismissed from the Abbey was to be allowed to stay in the Abbey guest house, nor in another Abbey which was poor. Instead he had to go to a monastery in another district where he would have his needs and where he would learn good conduct.

Abbot Stephen decided against overcrowding the monastery and estimated that thirty-five monks and fifty brothers would be adequate and that these numbers could not be exceeded without the Abbot's permission. From the Letter Book we learn that a monk and a brother had threatened to murder the Abbot because he had not given them permission to go somewhere. These monks were required to repent; if they did not they had to go to a monastery in another district. The year 1228 was a difficult year financially for the Abbey and we find Abbot Stephen commanding everyone through the power of the Holy Spirit to be moderate in every way, and to think about how the house could recover from its inestimable debt, in case that in the following year the monks would have to be dispersed — 'far from us may that be', remarked Stephen. Stephen then turned his attention to the granges and directed that an annual audit should be carried out to see if their profits were greater or less than their expenses.

Stephen also directed that no new buildings should be erected in the Cloister garth or in the courtyard of the grange buildings. Instead they should be erected along the East and West of the parallelogram, to secure against thievery and other dangers. Only the houses in the main monastery complex had to have good roofs. The secular clergy were not to be given nor receive rents without permission of the Father Abbot. The lay-brothers were not permitted to talk to the monks in the dining room, in the dormitory, nor in the infirmary, so that order could be maintained. Regarding the Abbey Church, the Cross over the High Altar had to be removed because the Image was hidden and wax candles were not to be used in the Sanctuary except on days when there was a special sermon in the Chapter. Stephen also reinforced the enclosure rules, by declaring that monks and brothers were not to go home to their parents or relatives, except on business on behalf of the Abbey. Neither the monks nor lay-brothers nor their relatives were to contrive reasons for such journeys. Any official of the monastery who gave such permission would be removed from office at the next Visitation. If he was not in office, then he would be the last man for a month on the procession and he would be whipped every Wednesday and Friday during that month.

Monks were entitled to have blood letting. For their health's sake they were advised to do so; a monk could only postpone such an operation if he had the consent of the Prior or the Infirmarian. Furthermore, if he postponed the operation he was not allowed to have it when he wished.

On a Feast Day the Convent Mass had to be said later than usual and the Office of the Dead had to be sung, with a pause between the verses. Stephen gave further directions about the Enclosure and commanded that the only way in and out of the monastery should be via 'the big gate near the kitchen'. Regarding meals, the sub-cellarer or any other monk was not to give an extra meal to anyone without special permission from the Abbot or the Prior or the Infirmarian. Anyone who did was to be whipped in Chapter the following day and be put on bread and water each time he did it. Furthermore the Prior and the Deputy Prior had to be watchful that no monk or lay-brother should receive a second meal unless he had need of it. No children were to be given holidays in the monastery, without a note and special permission from the Abbot. Anyone breaking this rule was to be the last man in the procession for a month, was to be put on bread and water every Friday and whipped in the Chapter during the same month.

Regarding Castle Grange, Stephen ordered that the carpenter had to be sent there before the Feast of All Saints, otherwise the Cellarer and the carpenter would be put on bread and water every Friday and whipped in Chapter until he went. The cobbler's shop, in which were made the shoes, belts, harness etc. had also to be moved to the same grange. Concerning the monks' dress, there was to be no deviation; only white cowls were to be worn. Stephen must have sensed some opposition to all his commands, for he declared that after he finished this Visitation if any lay-brother raised strife against these Decrees of the Order and did not repent, then he would be exiled to another district and not return to Duiske without the Abbot's permission. Again referring to the debt on the Abbey in 1228, Stephen asked that no house should be built on the granges except stables and animal sheds until the debt on the monastery was cleared and the monks' Chapter House and the kitchen of the guest house completed. Any monk who had to go home on business had to go on horseback, rather than on foot in order to avoid scandal. All monks and brothers had to give their wealth to the Abbot otherwise they would be expelled. Abbot Stephen was anxious to have good communication

within the Abbey. He wrote these instructions in Latin and he required that reference to the Rule of the Order should be made in French only, so that rebellious people cannot have a means of hiding their opposition and, that the visitors when they came would be understood and in turn would understand. If not the offender should be put on bread and water for a day with a whipping in Chapter. No one was to be accepted as a monk if he could not make his Confession in Latin or in French, whether he was an Irishman or a foreigner — no matter what nation he came from. All these directions which Stephen prepared had to be read aloud for two years at the meal known as the Collation so that no one could plead ignorance of them.

Regarding Confession, only the monk appointed by the Abbot was to hear Confessions. If anyone did this without the latter's permission then he was to be expelled. On the granges, the Cellarer had full control over the distribution of the entire crop of corn. No one was even allowed to leave a quantity of this aside for the brothers, without the Abbot's consent. If any monk should do this then he would be sent to another district. The same applied to any person who gave the monastery's cattle or money to lay people without the consent of the Abbot or the Cellarer.

In Ireland during this period there were what were known as double monasteries, that is a group of nuns and a group of monks under the direction of the same Abbot or Abbess. This was against the Cistercian rules and Stephen legislated that no one should ever be accepted as a nun in Duiske Abbey because of the disorderliness and the scandals which prevailed throughout Ireland because of this practice. However the Earl Marshal and other people complained about the nuns and Stephen ordered that a suitable place should be found for them before the Feast of Saint Michael, where they could build their own convent and live modestly. In the meantime Stephen prohibited any nun to live in the monastery and asked the community to 'await the Divine' — in other words not to be distracted from their Divine Vocation, while the nuns were living near the monastery.

No monk or brother was to hinder the Abbot's command or object to it, so that the Abbot could regulate the wealth of the house both internally and externally. If anyone broke this rule twice then he would be expelled without fail. The monastery had to obtain a copy of the new Book of Usages. If not, the Prior, the Deputy Prior and the Cantor should be put on bread and water as long as the monastery was without it. No land was permitted to be leased to local people without the agreement of the Abbot. If any official did this without the latter's consent then he would be dismissed from office and not be allowed to hold office for another five years. Choir monks who did this would be expelled and not allowed to return to the Abbey without the consent of the Abbot. Abbot Stephen decided that the Sub-Prior of the Abbey should be made master of the lay-brothers, so that good order could be maintained in the Abbey. At this time, there must have been conflict between Abbot Thomas and his Prior but the Prior was allowed to remain in office to see if his respect for the Rules of the Order and for the Abbot were satisfactory. Monks were not allowed to speak together, nor to each other, except in the presence of the Abbot or the Prior or the Infirmarian. If the brothers broke the silence then they were to be punished. Lay people were not allowed inside the Enclosure, nor permitted to help in the infirmary, the Abbey kitchens, or the infirmary kitchen to prepare meals. It was the supervisory duty of the Prior and Cellarer to see that this did not happen; if it did, then the Abbot had to

report this at the next General Chapter Meeting and the Prior and Cellarer had to fast every Friday whilst this was going on. Sick monks and sick lay-brothers were permitted to take their meals together in the infirmary, the only exception being the blind and those confined to bed. From 1228 the monks were asked to work harder than they had up to then and they were not allowed to do private work. Every monk had to take his turn at 'beating the board' at 2 a.m. to awaken the monks. The board was two wooden clappers held together by a cord and no monk could be dispensed from this duty except by the Abbot in Chapter. These clappers or boards are still used on the last two days of Holy Week in modern monasteries, when no bells are rung.

One third of the monks' jumpers, cloaks and sandals had to be given to the Porter before the Feast of Saint Martin for distribution to the poor. The Infirmarian was not allowed to speak to two monks together but to one only in an appointed place. If he broke the rule then he would receive punishment for breaking the silence.

Stephen also felt it necessary to reinforce his directions on drinking, because of the disorderliness that might arise, so he directed that no monk or brother should go into the dining room between the normal drinking hours and dinner at 4 p.m. in summer, or between lunch, the mid-day meal, and Vespers in winter for more than one drink, unless accompanied by the Abbot. He also enforced the law against women with no monk allowed to speak alone to a woman at the monastery gate. If he did he was to be the last man in the procession and receive a whipping in the Chapter once a week until the next Visitation. Repeating the dangers of drinking Abbot Stephen directed that neither monk nor lay-brother, should take food or drink within three leagues of the monastery or the granges, nor were they allowed to accept the hospitality of country people without the Abbot's permission which would be rarely given. Returning to the monks' dress, the brothers and monks were not allowed to wear belts which were foppishly sewn. A lay-brother living on a grange was not allowed to accept a drink other than in the refectory of the grange, no matter who offered it to him or in what place he was offered it unless the Abbot was present. If any monk broke this rule then he would be given water as his only drink for forty days. Regarding the singing of Psalms, Abbot Stephen declared that these should be sung as Saint Bernard wished, in plain chant and not in two part harmony. Any pair who sang in two parts had to be split up, put on bread and water the next day and be whipped in Chapter. Regarding the diet of the monks, all monks and lay-brothers were to have the same menu, except in cases of certain types of illness. Fish was not to be served on three consecutive days instead of eggs and vegetables. Only one vegetable dish was to be served at each meal except during bloodletting or Visitation. If this was broken then the Prior, the Sub-Prior, the Cellarer and the Deputy Cellarer were to be put on bread and water for three consecutive days and given a whipping in the Chapter for a week and be allowed no dishes of eggs and vegetables whilst being punished.

Another reference was then made to the buildings, this time to the buildings outside the gate. Stephen declared that they were either to be repaired or demolished before the Feast of All Saints, in case the monastery would be brought into ill repute. If the matter was not cleared up then the Cellarer and the porter were to be put on bread and water every Friday until the next Visitation.

One of the characteristics of Cistercian houses was and still is hospitality. In Medieval days, the pilgrims or travellers usually arrived on foot or on horseback. In 1228 Abbot Stephen advised that the stable inside the monastery yard should be closed for a while, because of the 'inestimable expense on the house and the great peril to souls'. Abbot Stephen advised that fine cloaks or foppish cloaks were not to be given to the lay-brothers. If this should occur then he who gave them and he who received them should be put on bread and water every Friday and be whipped in the Chapter. Those who had them already were to give them up to the wardrobe keeper in the presence of the Abbot or the Master of the lay-brothers. Returning to buildings Stephen advised that the Cellarer should supply enough lead to put a roof on the Northern part of the Church and that the tombs in the window of the Chapter house had to be taken out and placed elsewhere. In the refectory the lay-brothers were to use pottery cups and not pewter ones, similarly the monks were not allowed to have silver-plated cups in their refectory. However, if a pottery cup was broken it was permissible to mend it with silver wire only. Relations between the lay-brothers and monks were also explained. The lay-brothers were not to ask to be on a level with the monks, especially those lay-brothers who because of their work had contact with the monks in the refectory. However, they were to have share in any extra dishes available. A lay-brother was not allowed to hinder a monk, through pulling his sleeve or harassing him, if he did then he was to be without an extra dish of any kind for a full week.

Stephen returned to the buildings at the gate, and decided that it was not to be used as an altar or chapel, but should be finished. For the infirmary a good supply of linen had to be provided for the poor and the sick, as well as suitable meals and better drink than usual. However, any lay-brother other than one in the infirmary who took a meal without his cloak on should be whipped at the Chapter for each of three days and also be put on bread and water. No lay person was to take a drink in the infirmary nor in the refectory unless the Abbot was present or at the Abbot's special request. No one was to serve a meal using silver cups, or cups with silver feet, or with silver spoons. No monk or brother was to have a purse or pocket knife, except notaries and officers who required them by nature of their office. Anyone who had these should be given water as his drink until he gave them up. No local person was to receive food in the kitchen of the infirmary, otherwise the monk infirmarian and the brother infirmarian would be put on bread and water. Any monks travelling on horseback, or living on the grange, had to keep the silence whilst journeying otherwise they would be punished for breaking the silence. It was customary for the porter to sit on a high stool at the gate, and Stephen forbade that he should have a bed in the gate house. The Master of the lay-brothers had to visit the granges every five weeks, to see how they were progressing and to correct any disorder that there might be. (This meant that he had to go to Killenny, Grange Cuffe, Annamult, Old Grange and Monks' Grange in rotation.) The lay-brothers who had a monk appointed to help them in their duties were not to frustrate him in his efforts, but to follow his instructions after he had consulted them. The shoemaker brother was not to supply sandals to any monk or brother or anyone else without permission from the Abbot or Cellarer or from another monk appointed by the Abbot. The lay-brothers were further exhorted to have respect for the monks and especially for the Cellarer; otherwise they were to be punished.

Graignamanagh and the Papacy

The Cistercian troubles in Ireland did not escape the notice of the papacy: the Irish problem was always discussed at the Cistercian General Chapter. Nevertheless the monastic life seems to have settled a lot. The visitations were carried out in the prescribed fashion, although there were occasional outbursts of violence as at Monasterevan and Jerpoint when two monks were blinded,[1] at Fermoy where an abbot was killed,[2] at Inishlounaght where a lay-brother was killed [3] and at Corcumroe where in 1231 the Cistercian visitor from Furness was refused admission.[4] When this happened the General Chapter had to appeal to Gregory IX and it is likely that the General Chapter received this disturbing news from Abbot Thomas of Graignamanagh. Gregory IX had to ask King Henry III and the Justiciar to bring the guilty to justice and protect Cistercian visitors.[5]

However, the handling of this affair must not have damaged the reputation of Abbot Thomas of Graignamanagh for in 1240 Gregory IX issued a mandate to the 'Archbishop of Cashel, the Abbot of Graigue and the Abbot of Jerpoint to enquire and report back to him on the signification of the Archbishop elect of Armagh, that when he was called by Olto, Cardinal of St Nicholas in Carcere, Papal legate, to preside over that Church, he found it more stripped of its goods by the prelates and barons of those parts than could be believed and among them by his own suffragans of whom the late bishop of Clogher was the worst of his persecutors. The late Archbishop of Armagh going to the Pope obtained letters to the said legate ordering him to revoke all processes and if no composition could be effected to bring the cause to an end. The bishop of Clogher being dead, petition is made for the Union of the Churches.' [6]

This mandate must have been successfully carried out as there is no further mention of it in the Papal Registers. In 1400 Boniface IX sent a mandate to David Cornwalshe, Abbot of Graignamanagh, asking him to collate and assign to John Smyth, Rector of Kilmedy in the diocese of Ossory, if found fit after examination, the canonry and prebend of Blacratin, value not exceeding ten marks, which became void and reserved to the Apostolic see through Pope Gregory IX's promotion of Alexander Balscot Bishop of Meath to the see of Ossory.[7] Apparently this man was not consecrated as Gregory IX and his successor Urban VI died without having accomplished this. However Smyth was to hold the Church, value not exceeding two marks.

In 1444 Abbot Philip of Duiske received a Papal Mandate. This time the Pope had been informed by Patrick Macaluard, a canon of St Mary's, Roscommon, that Thomas Odrefyn, Abbot of the Augustinian monastery of St Mary, Ferns, had 'delapidated goods thereof, committed perjury and on account of these and other crimes is defamed in those parts. If Patrick who has made his profession and who, before entering religion was dispensed by Papal authority as the son of a priest and unmarried woman to be promoted to all, even holy, orders and receive and hold the deanery of Ferns of which provision was ordered to be made to him and who, from fear of Thomas' power, cannot safely meet him within the diocese of Ferns, will accuse Thomas before them etc as usual to deprive him and in what event to make provision of the said monastery value not exceeding twenty-four marks sterling to Patrick, whether it become void by such deprivation or be void by the death of Nicholas Odrufyn or in any other way. The Pope hereby dispenses him to exercise the administration etc and grants that he may be blessed by any Catholic Bishop.'[8] This case was not settled however and Abbot Philip was succeeded by Abbot Dermit.

In the CPL 1447 there is a petition or confirmation of a Papal Mandate to Dermit, Abbot of Duiske, giving possession of the Abbey to Thomas.[9] This was necessary because Dermit was not at peace in possession of the abbey and there was opposition to him. Probably after the retired abbot Philip died the succession was disputed.

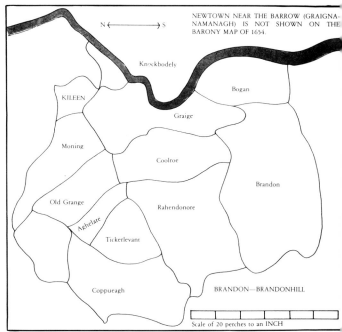

On the Barony Map of 1654 Graige is mentioned. In a Charter, Geoffrey Fitz Robert gave up all claim to this land. On the Modern Map Tinna Park, Newtown, Priest's Valley, Ballyduff, Bohermore, Coolfearnamanagh have been carved out of Graige and Brandon 1654 is now Brandon Hill, Ballynakill, Deerpark.

The Abbey and the Town

We must now turn our attention to Graigna-managh. How did this word come to signify Duiske Abbey? There are those who interpret Graigna-managh as Graig-na-mbreathnach (the Village of the Welsh) because of the Welsh colonists who came here or Graig-na managh because of the monks who settled here. One mile west of the abbey is Old Grange, the monks' temporary accommodation as the abbey was being built. Some of its ruins still exist. The walls are four feet thick and form buttresses as they rise from the ground.

Duiske Abbey's site was two acres great measure and according to Mills in his Account Roll of Holy Trinity Dublin, the 'acre in the Pale corresponded to two and a half modern statute acres'. Therefore the abbey complex of 'Church, cemetery, cloister, orchard and garden was 5 acres in extent'.[1] The Cistercians were bound to the Rules of Enclosure and a perimeter wall was always built around the abbey complex. No trace of this Enclosure wall is visible today but there is an interesting record of c. 1875 which states that near the west gable of the Abbey Church there stood fifty years ago an ancient wall 20ft high and 8 ft thick with two vaulted cellars at its base. It was removed when new houses and the Abbey Hotel in the Main Street were being built. When knocking down this wall the workmen undermined one end of it and tried to pull it down with ropes but so firm was the bond of the mortar that instead of toppling over as they expected, the whole mass of masonry 'sat down', as an eye witness described it, 'in one solid block on the part under-mined'.[2] We must remember that Main Street, and the Bridge (c. 1750) near Chapel Street did not exist in the monastic period. If an enclosure area of 530ft x 530ft is delineated, then it is possible that the houses in Main Street are built on the foundations of the enclosure wall. This mass of masonry over the two vaulted chambers may have been the main entrance to the abbey complex. The porter who answered the door would have occupied an alcove in the wall. Here he sat on a stool and the two vaulted rooms may have been Cellars, or reception rooms underneath this Gateway just as at Mellifont. Furthermore the route from Kilkenny and Ullard southwards would have converged on this door. When we walk from the Barrow River, up Main Street and down Chapel Street and Barrow Lane are we not walking within the former monastic enclosure? Up to about twenty years ago all funerals to Duiske Abbey traversed this route to reach the Abbey Church. It is said to have been discontinued during an influenza epidemic at that time when many people died.

Reference to the modern map will show the Newtown of Graigue lying north west of the monastery complex with Tinna Park and Priest's Valley on the west and Coolfearnamanagh (the monk's wood) on the east. However references to the Barony Map of 1654 and comparison with the modern Townland

Index shows that these along with Deer Park were carved out of the area known as 'Graigue'. However the *Nova Villa* iuxta Barrow was on the Carlow side of the River — and this *Nova Villa* or *New Town* was carved out of a townland called *Carra Varra*, two fields of which remain to designate the latter. In this townland on rising ground there is an Old Church site, from which Duiske Abbey is distinctly visible. To the north of this townland are the two remaining fields known as Carra-Varra. In these two fields and west of the Old Church site are two major earthworks from which the fields radiate in long strips, as though sub-divided and distributed by the early settlers. They do not indicate the usual patch work quilt field pattern of Ireland.

Early grants made to new towns in the Middle Ages were on large tracts of land near the sea, for example the Louthside of Drogheda, Dundalk, Limerick, Rosponte, Wexford, or near great rivers as at Kilkenny, Inistiogue, Jerpoint or Graignamanagh. These tracts of land were granted to people for habitation. In the early grants made to these privileged towns they are called 'Frankes Dones', or free gifts. The first and most essential of these Frankesdones was the free gift of the ground on which the town was erected. This parcel of land was set aside as privileged places, freedoms or boroughs. The size of these tracts was usually not big enough for military or knights' service. A rent in money was arranged instead for each tenement into which the ground might be sub-divided or a gross sum for an entire tract, made payable by the occupiers, their heirs and successors for ever.

Nova Villa iuxta Barrow, Newtown Graignamanagh, or Newtown alias Carravarra, on the Co. Carlow side of the river, is shown in relationship to the modern electoral division of Newtown on the Co. Kilkenny side of the river Barrow, indicated by arrow.

Newtown iuxta Barrow — Newtown on the Co Carlow side of the River Barrow from the air.

Site of Castle at Newtown looking north east.

It was the custom in England for the Normans to place towns on the perimeter of parishes. In Ireland certain examples may be cited wherein towns were placed on the edge of the monastery's estate — such places as Newtown, Jerpoint (Jerpoint Abbey), Collon (Mellifont Abbey), Tristernagh (Tristernagh Abbey), Inistiogue (Inistiogue Abbey) and Newtown iuxta Barrow. Graignamanagh was no excep-

Section of double bank enclosure in Newtown.

tion. It was also the practice of the colonists to carve out homesteads and small holdings and then bring the settlers to occupy them, rather like the modern advanced factory scheme where the factory is built first and then the tenant is found.

Once a colonist took up residence his rights were guaranteed, rights that may have been acquired through marriage, apprenticeship or direct grant.

Entrance to stone faced enclosure taken from the bank.

The same entrance taken from the adjoining field.

When the monks came to build Duiske Abbey they brought their tradesmen with them. The Charters recall Thomas the Mason,[3] Stephen the Mason,[4] Henry, son of Donald the carpenter,[5] Thomas the baker,[6] Peter the miller,[7] Adam la Taverner,[8] Henry la Taverner,[9] (only a burgess could keep a tavern) and Henry the barber [10] — who must have been a barber-cum-surgeon for the bloodletting practices of those times. Indeed in 1228 during his Visitation of Duiske Abbey, Stephen de Lexington advised that this practice should be done according to Cistercian directions. If anyone postponed his turn, without giving a satisfactory explanation to the Prior or the Infirmarian, then he would not have a new appointment arranged for him. There were other residents too for whom no occupation is mentioned such as Robert Fitzhugh,[11] Fitz Robert,[12] Fitzsinnot,[13] Alan Fitzmils,[14] Thomas Fitz Odo,[15] Peter le Rous,[16] Dermot Connartact,[17] and Conechor Ohekyr,[18] Andrew Tannur,[19] in all some eighteen families. Those employed in building the abbey only lived about one mile, (as the crow flies) from it.

The burgesses of these new towns were empowered to make free-holders out of their tenements to the extent of twenty feet and these free holders had rights of common with them. Each burgess was given three acres and he could carve this up. All burgess holders paid the same rent, in Dundalk 12d,[20] Limerick 12d,[21] Inistiogue 12d,[22] Wexford 12d [23] and for Newtown iuxta Barrow there is a lease by 'Henry son and heir of Adam Tabernar (the taverner) to the convent of Duiske of a burgage in Newtown lying between the two highways from their Crossing the highway from Idrone and across the Barrow, the rent 12d to be paid to [24] the overlord at Easter and Michaelmas.'

The burgesses also possessed certain privileges. They could demise and alienate such property as they wished and they had the privilege of having their own court. The Charters of Duiske provide an interesting example of this when the Widow Sybl and her daughter Susan transferred the following properties to Duiske Abbey: 'Thomas the baker rented 7 acres from her at Drummenbeythe and Adam Connachbath for two virgates of land between the burage of Dermot Connachtath for two virgates of land of the aforesaid Michael and halfpenny from Peter le Rous who rented a house from her in Newtown for 12p. All of these she grants to the monastery.' [25]

The tradesmen in Graignamanagh spent over twenty years building the monastery church and probably grew to like the place. In time the village prospered and by 1280 they had a provost called Eliya.[26] In 1291 the Abbot of Duiske, Brother John, became attorney for three years and it is learned from the Justiciary Rolls that in 1306 the Justiciar presided at the court in Graignamanagh.[27]

Another law relating to new towns in the Middle Ages was that merchants and visitors had to reside in the town for forty days. The burgesses were exempted from lastage, pontage, and passage which was fortunate for this riverside settlement. The Abbey of Duiske was the local bank for Newtown Graignamanagh. Records show that a similar practice operated in Chester Abbey, England and Quarre Abbey on the Isle of Wight. In Deed 87 there is an acknowledgement by Richard de St Florence and William his brother, 'that they have received from the abbot and convent of Duiske a box containing muniments which have been in the custody of the said convent'. Medieval monasteries were usually walled and the streets were paved with stones. Barrow Lane and Clurnagh Lane may have been such streets. Clurnagh derives its name from Clocharnach — because of its stoney character. It is very steep and crosses Killeen Hill and Baurnavidaun.

Site of Newtown Co. Carlow looking west and the Graveyard at the Medieval Church site of Kylmohenenoth.

Notice the Forts and the Old Church site. Carravarra is designated by two fields. This is all that remains of this former townland from which Newtown near the Barrow was carved. This is one mile from Duiske Abbey.

The tree trunk signifying the graveyard area which farmers still avoid today.

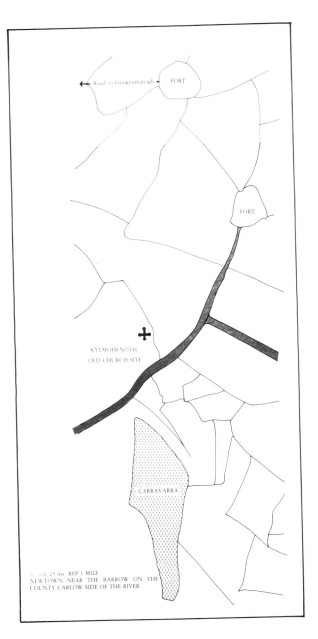

Road to Graignamanagh — FORT

FORT

✝

KYLMOHENOTH
OLD CHURCH SITE

CARRAVARRA

25 … 25 ms. REP 1 MILE
NEWTOWN NEAR THE BARROW ON THE
COUNTY CARLOW SIDE OF THE RIVER

This was perhaps the ancient way from Duiske Abbey to Ullard and Barrowmount. Today the surface of Clurnagh Lane is metalled with tar-macadam, but approaching the Abbey from the east, on the right hand side of the present main road is a lane called Blindlane some two miles from the abbey and this is a medieval pavement as shown in the photograph. It is about 10ft wide and goes straight up to Killeen Hill to join Clurnagh Lane. This was probably the route taken by the monks from the Abbey to the fishing weir at Castle Ford.

Pathway to fisheries at Graignamanagh.

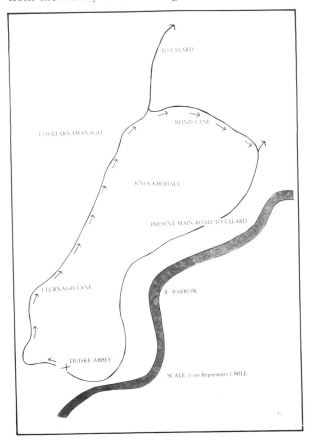

Monastic Pathway

Mareschal (or Marshal) William,
Earl of Pembroke and Striguil,
1146-1219, founder of Duiske
Abbey
[illustration courtesy of Longmans, London.]

The Knight of Duiske Abbey

Duiske Abbey has a crosslegged thirteenth centu figure of a knight in armour. Unfortunately when workmen were lowering the gable of the North transept in 1813 the effigy was broken. Three facts are known: (i) he is a knight, (ii) the period is the thirteenth century, (iii) he must have been a man of importance. Documentary evidence supports Alan Beg, Elias de Prendergast or John le Poer. Let us examine the possibilities. Alan is Alan Beg (small), or Alan petit. In 1224, Alan with permission of his heiress (his daughter Cecilia) gave to the convent of Duiske (in the Abbey of which he chooses a burial place for himself) of half the church of Ullard, *viz*, all its tithes from his holdings in that vill. This is the only extant record of a gift in exchange for a sepulchral plot in Duiske Abbey.[1] Alan witnessed charters to St Thomas' Abbey, Dublin and to St Mary's Abbey in 1202. His colleague was Ralph the rector of Gowran who witnessed this charter and one for St Thomas' Abbey, Dublin. Ralph's own tombstone, a huge slab with the recumbent effigy of an ecclesiastic in vestments is still seen in Gowran Church. He died in 1253.[2] The example of Ralph may have inspired Alan to make a similar gesture. The only information lacking is the declaration that he was a Knight, I cannot find 'Alan le petit Knight' written anywhere in the documents.

Now we come to Elias. The case for this sculpture being an effigy of Elias may be supported as follows: Philip de Prendergast was the son of Maurice de Prendergast, from the Flemish colony in

Alan Beg, crossed legged in the manner of a Crusader. He gave half the tithes of Ullard accruing to him from his tenants in that townland in exchange for a burial place in Duiske Abbey.

Pembrokeshire, one of William Marshal's men who married Matilda de Quency in 1198, and thus became lord of the manor of Enniscorthy.[3] He died in 1229. The next Prendergast we meet in the document is William de Prendergast witnessing a charter to Duiske in 1230.[4] In 1259, Elias son of Richard de Prendergast Knight[5] is mentioned and in 1280 Elias becomes Provost of Newtown (Nova Villa),[6] 'in other words the Mayor of the town. By the turn of the century Elias had died and knighthood was a hereditary office. In the Justiciary Rolls there is mention of the circuit judge, the Justiciar, presiding over a court in Graignamanagh in 1306. At the court a man named John Hay of Athbolsy and another man Michael Myagh were accused of killing Henry McMorgh in the town of Ferns and robbing him, even though he had been promised safe custody by the Justiciar to the Court. What is interesting as far as our study of Graignamanagh is concerned, is the panel of jurors consisting of two knights, William son of Elias former provost (second generation) and Nicholas Auenel and the freeholders Richard Whithay, Philip Bossher, Philip son of Robert Furlong, Walter de Lou, Nicholas de Baunford, John le Clerk of Ferns, John Turneronde, Stephen le Chapman Nich? son of Richard Furlong and William son of Simon.[7] This establishes that Newtown (Nova Villa) had a family called Prendergast who were very much involved with Duiske Abbey, secondly that they were knights in the thirteenth century and thirdly one of them as Mayor of the town may have merited such a tombstone.

The third possibility is John — John le Poer, a knight who became a monk in the abbey, and who was murdered on his way to Dunbrody.[8] However it is hardly likely that a Cistercian monk would have had his effigy carved like this. The Order would have frowned on such an act.

Therefore the effigy must be that of either Alan

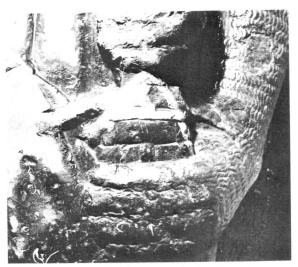

Detail of hands holding sword showing the mark 'A' on Duiske Abbey Effigy.

Beg c. 1220 or the Provost Elias 1280 (knight). However an examination of the seal of the Charter of Alan Beg depicts Alan as a knight[9] in a suit of mail on horseback. Therefore from the available evidence we may argue the case for the effigy as representing Alan Beg as follows: he gave the donation of half the income of the Church of Ullard to Duiske Abbey in exchange for a burial plot there, secondly he lived around c. 1229, thirdly his colleague the Rector of Gowran had made a similar arrangement and fourthly the evidence of a Knight on a charger on his seal supports his being a Knight. I cannot find any other request for a sepulchral plot in the documents for Duiske Abbey, other than that of Alan Beg's.

There is a postscript to this evidence however. One evening I was looking at the photograph of this effigy and there carved in stone on the top of the scabbard was the Initial 'A' — Alan... I was overjoyed.

Caring for the People

The Rule of St Benedict demands that a special interest should be taken in poor people and the Guest master has a special function in looking after them. All Cistercian Abbeys had a Guest house for travellers and an infirmary in cases of sudden illness. According to the Annals of Duiske the monks of Graignamanagh had to deal with two major outbreaks of disease. The first was in 1316 when smallpox broke out near Dunbrody and there was a shortage of food in that district. Henry the Abbot sent John le Poer, a monk, and Gilbert Wengum, a lay-brother, and an Irish boat boy went with supplies to Dunbrody Abbey. It was loaded with meal, a firkin of butter, a cheese, a barrel of cider and a cask of wine. However it is recorded that when the boat reached Coolraney Wood, it was robbed by Mac Collatyn, who slew the monks and sank the boat, the only one escaping being the boat boy who swam across the river. However the anecdote shows the readiness, willingness and generosity of the monks in supplying those in need. [1]

In 1347 the plague known as the Black Death appeared in Europe and reached England in July 1348, first apparently in Dorsetshire, spreading through Somerset and Devon and north eastwards to London, and then throughout the country. Bristol was a great centre for Anglo-Irish trade at this time. In 1172 Henry II granted to 'his men of Bristol his city of Dublin with all liberties and free usages which they have at Bristol and throughout the land'.[2] It was probably from Bristol that the Plague reached Ireland, appearing at Howth and Drogheda at the beginning of August, though the timing of the outbreak is so close to that of the outbreak in Europe that it may possibly have come direct from the continent.

The Diary of the Franciscan Friar Clyn of Kilkenny tells us that the cities of Dublin and Drogheda were almost destroyed and wasted of men, so that in Dublin alone from the beginning of August to Christmas fourteen thousand men died. The mortality in the towns was very great and in 1351 the jurors of an inquisition said that in the time of the said pestilence the greater part of the citizens of Cork and other faithful men of the King dwelling there, went the way of all flesh. In Lent 1349, the plague reached Kilkenny and by 6 March eight of the Friar's Preachers were already dead. The plague struck Lower Ossory and people used to come to St Mullins on pilgrimage, some with votive offerings, some to wade the waters, asking for their preservation from the plague or 'galar dhu'. In the same year it reached Graignamanagh Abbey. It eased off for a while in the winter months, but then raged again in the hot months. Many people came to the abbey for help, covered in sores and spitting blood. By 1350 the plague had abated, but many of the monks who helped in the infirmary died, others became very weak so that within the monastery Abbot Henry had to relax the rule. Nocturnes were discontinued because the brethren weakened by illness and labour in the infirmary were unable to attend them.

Gradually the monks returned to health and dispensed hospitality to the poor again. A lay-brother, Simon Brown sometimes called Fuseus or Riabhach or Reagh Swarthy, came from Mellifont Abbey to Graignamanagh. He was, according to the Annals of Duiske, a man learned in *Scientia herborium*. He enlarged the garden and planted many fruit trees. In the Garth he set flowers and sweet scented shrubs and in the centre he raised a noble sun dial. It is also recorded that when he came from Mellifont he brought with him a yew branch, which he planted in the abbot's garden behind the infirmary where it flourished for over four hundred years. The stump of this yew tree remains in the vicinity of the Abbey. Yew trees were popular in Medieval Abbeys. From them crossbows were made, as the yew tree wood contained very few knots and being very flexible, was suitable for bow making. The arrows were sharpened on a sandstone. According to the Calendar of Papal Letters on 23 August 1460, Philip Walch, a monk of Duiske had gone out with a fellow monk to a place within the precinct of the monastery appointed by the abbot and monks for archery as a pastime when a little boy ran into the line of fire and was killed by Brother Philip who was shooting at a target. A similar block for sharpening arrow heads may be seen in Mellifont Abbey whilst the famous mural in Holy Cross Abbey, depicts an archer with his bow and arrow in a hunting scene. Today the herb called Pellitory grows profusely on the abbey walls. Stewed in ale it is claimed to be a remedy for curing gravel in the kidney and on the slopes of Brandon the Sun Dew *Drosera Rotunda* Folio grows and cooked in ale is the elixir for those who seek eternal youth.

Tomb at Duiske Abbey

David the Harper: the Ballyogan Cross.

The Harp that Once...

Within the precincts of Duiske Abbey is a wheel cross known as the Ballyogan Cross. One of the carvings depicts David with his harp. It is an unusual harp as it is without a front support or rest and is in fact a cruit or harp that was played with a bow, rather than having its strings plucked. In researching the charters of Abbey of Duiske I found that in 1278 there was a Quit Claim by Raymond Roche, lawyer, on behalf of David, son of Stephen the 'Harpur', concerning the holding of Coppenagh to the convent of Duiske for six silver marks.[1] These harpers were bards, who came from Gloucestershire to Ireland as Anglo-Norman adventurers.[2] They built Harperstown Castle, near Taghmon Co Wexford. Whether there is any connection between this memorial cross and this family is not known. Nevertheless this bowed harp once aroused the interest of a group of Welsh harpists, who came to Duiske to inspect it.[3]

The harp played by Aengus, monk of Holy Cross Abbey was also a cruit or bowed harp. The Annals of Duiske describe how this Brother Aengus of Holy Cross Abbey instructed 'my Lord Milo Roch, the Bishop of Leighlin, who is master of many instruments. Aengus repaired the Old wind organ which not having been used of late years was sadly affected by damp and its bellows gnawed by rats. But he hath remedied these defects and now it sounds full mellow and blends wondrous sweet with the choir voices. In truth Aengus excels in music any citharist or harpers overheard in these parts for not alone is he versed in psalms and choir basses (witness his setting of Benedicam Dominum) but he is even a cunning performer on the cruit (the bowed harp). Withal my Lord the Abbot, looks not favourably on this harping, for of an evening when he thrums his munster fownns (i.e. phonn = Foinn = tunes) wild but strangely sweet — the brethren are apt to forget Complain.' Of the Musician Aengus, Dowlyng says, '*Inter bardos mumeratur pro omnibus instrumentis*' and Ware says that 'he was more addicted to the story of musick and poetry than was fit'. The organs were still in the Abbey at the time of the dissolution.

However the harp features in another story of Duiske Abbey. Along the River Barrow there are many castles, one of which was Poulmounty Castle, home of Cahir mor Mac Kavanagh and another Coolkyle, home of Gilbert de La Roche. The former had a daughter Eilleen, who had promised to marry Mac Caomh Insi Cneamha, better known as Carol O'Daly, youngest brother of Donogh More O'Daly, who was Lord Abbot of Boyle (in 1244).[4] The O'Dalys were famous and important people in Connaught, and Abbot O'Daly was one of the most accomplished men of his time and particularly excelled in music, being often referred to as the Ovid of Ireland.[5]

O'Daly went to France to a gathering of Bards, but was away for over a year and Eilleen thought

Poulmounty and the River Barrow — 'Eilleen Aroon country'.

that he would not be returning. In the meantime Cathair Mor O'Kavanagh thought that his daughter should marry Philip de La Roche of Coulkyle Castle. Gilbert de La Roche also knew that if he married Eilleen, then he would secure the Kavanagh landed possessions as well. Eilleen agreed to marry Philip de La Roche and the day was fixed for the wedding. On the eve of the wedding there was a party. Carol O'Daly had heard about the intended marriage and hurried back from France. O'Daly as a harper gained access among the crowd at the pre-wedding party and it so happened that he was called upon by Eilleen to play his harp. 'It was then, touching his harp with all the pathetic sensibility which the interesting occasion inspired, he infused his own feelings into the song he had composed and breathed into his 'softened strain' the very soul of pensive melody.'[6] The translation and interpretation we must leave to Hardiman.

'In the first stanza he intimates, according to the Irish idiom, that he would walk with her, that is that he would be her partner or only love for life. In the second he says that he would entertain her, and afford her every delight. After this he asks if she will depart with him or in the impressive manner of the original, "Wilt thou stay, or wilt thou come with me, Eileen a Roon." She soon felt the force of this tender appeal, and replied in the affirmative; on which, in an ecstasy of delight, he bursts forth into his "hundred thousand welcomes". To reward his fidelity and affection, his fair one contrived to go with him "that every night".'[7]

Carol O'Daly and Eilleen slipped away by boat and reached Duiske Abbey, at a spot where the Abbey Hotel stands today. There they were admitted by the Porter, and the Prior (David de Courcey) came out to see them. The Prior knew Carol O'Daly as brother of the Abbot of Boyle, Co

Roscommon, and they told the Prior of their desire to marry although Eilleen's father Cahir Mc Art O'Kavanagh wanted her to marry de la Roche. The Abbot agreed and they were married in Duiske Abbey. As soon as the wedding was performed, Gilbert de la Roche in anger reached the Abbey. However Gilbert knew the law of sanctuary that prevailed in Cistercian monasteries and the Prior took him aside and talked to him. Gilbert de la Roche was invited to stay at the abbey, the prior telling him that his niece Joan de Courcey would be coming that week. In due time Gilbert de la Roche married Joan de Courcey.

It is claimed that O'Daly lived and worked as a tenant on the estate. When Cahir Mac Art O'Kavanagh fell very ill, he sent for Eilleen to return and take possession of Poulmonty Castle and its lands. She did and she and her husband lived there for many years and were later buried side by side in St Moling's Churchyard. Little did Eilleen know that one day her great-grandson would be Abbot Kavanagh who would surrender the Abbey at the dissolution.

Regarding the authenticity of this legend certain facts can be established. The De La Roche and Kavanagh families did live in this district. A Gilbert de La Roche is referred to in Clyn's Annals and, as already mentioned, the O'Dalys were famous Connaught bards. Furthermore it was possible for the Abbot of Duiske to perform the wedding ceremony. As 'Rector of Duiske' he appointed a monk to serve the laity in the secular church.

This chapter opened with David The Harper and now it will close with David the Cantor who was the famous Cantor, David Trully, professed in France in 1825, and one of the monks who accompanied Dom Vincent on his return to Ireland in 1844. Four years later David the Cantor died from jaundice. Two metres from the Memorial Cross depicting

The Poulmounty River enters on the right. Coolhill Castle overlooks the left bend at the top of the stream here.

David the Harper is a memorial headstone to the relatives of David the Cantor of Mount Mellerey — a splendid continuity link in Cistercian Monasticism in Duiske Abbey.

The Dissolution

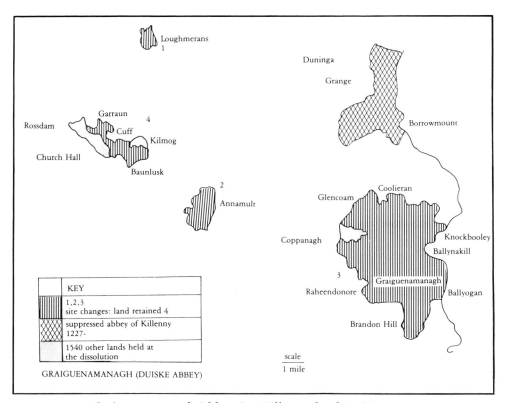

KEY

	1,2,3 site changes: land retained 4
	suppressed abbey of Killenny 1227-
	1540 other lands held at the dissolution

GRAIGUENAMANAGH (DUISKE ABBEY)

scale
1 mile

Graiguenamanagh Abbey Co. Kilkenny lands held c. 1541

Due to the great dearth of original source material we know very little about the ordinary life of the Irish monks. Stephen de Lexington's thirteen point plan improved monastic life in Ireland in the thirteenth century. However all was not well in fifteenth century Ireland. A letter written by the Abbot of Mellifont in 1497 to Jean de Cirey, Abbot of Citeaux, makes a list of complaints about the state of Cistercian monasticism. He told the Abbot of Citeaux that for a full hundred years no-one from the more remote districts had visited his father abbot and for this very reason many of the monasteries being left without a visitor and recognising no superior had, abbots and monks alike, gone over completely to the rebels. Abbot Troy blamed the decline as being due to the ceaseless wars which had ranged between the two races in Ireland as a result of the Norman conquest, the systems of provisions and commends made by the Holy See, the excessive oppression practised by the nobles, the pensions and tributes paid by monasteries for the support of provisors and commendatory abbots contrary to the rights of the incumbents as well as similar pensions and tributes for the support of the said incumbents against the provisors and commendatory abbots. In consequence of such exactions the Order was in straitened circumstances, and large sums of money for these and other purposes had to be poured out. Laymen had taken over the revenues of the monasteries so that the monks had not the wherewithal to live and were compelled to wander about in search of the very necessaries of life. Consequently hospitality was no longer practised, divine worship was neglected and many monks, throwing off the religious habit, lived among the nobility while the provisor and commendatory abbots took no care of the goods of the house except to plunder them for their own use.[1] Accordingly in 1306 we find Abbot Henry and the Convent of Duiske asking the General Chapter to petition the faithful for alms for the monastery 'then reduced to a lamentable state of dissolution by hostile incursions'.[2]

As has been mentioned, plagues broke out in Ireland, smallpox in 1316 and the Black Death in 1348. The numbers in the monastery dwindled, recruitment was difficult and many men who would have entered the Cistercian Order as lay brothers now joined the Mendicant Orders such as the Franciscans and the Friars of St Augustine. Furthermore not all abbots were good managers. In 1356 Abbot David Cornwalshe was fined £40 for harbouring Melaghin, son of Ph McOwen, O Bryan and others who had robbed and burned in the King's territory of Dublin, Kildare, Carlow and Wexford. They were also accused of murdering Edmund Trahern, Sheriff of Carlow. Abbot Cornwalshe received these men in Duiske Abbey where he 'entertained them with bread, drink, fish and clothes'. The Abbot was also accused of harbouring Richard Browne, David, son of Henry Duff, and other men who had committed many robberies. In the same year William Porter, Robert Hechyn, Henry Roth, John Eyhvard, John Brown and Richard Godman, who were monks robbed Abbot Cornwalshe's predecessor Abbot William Archer and stole from him two horses, value sixty shillings, one cloak, value ten shillings, one seal, value twenty shillings and sundry other goods and chattels worth five shillings. Even though Abbot Cornwalshe knew this he entertained these robber monks at Duiske Abbey.

This was very bad for the finances of Duiske Abbey, which could not afford such fines. In 1357 an appeal was made to the King at Westminster for forgiveness. 'Whereas the abbey of Duiske in Ireland is situated on the frontier of the King's Irish enemies and his said enemies pursuing his lieges in his peace there are oft times received in the abbey and are nourished therefrom although against the will of the abbot, and whereas the abbot was indicted before John de Boulton, late justice in that land, of the receiving of the King's enemies and of the bringing of victuals to them for their refreshment for pardon whereof he made fine before the said John by £40 and by various adversities coming upon him and the abbey he is now so depressed that he cannot pay the fine without the ruin of his estate, the King out of compassion has pardoned the fine, and acquits him thereof and by these presents makes restitution to him of all his goods fallen into the King's hand on account of the promise.'

By the middle of the fifteenth century, lettered

laymen began to interfere with the internal affairs of Duiske Abbey so much that in 1450 Abbot Dermit complained to the Holy See that James Butler, Earl of Ormond, and certain other nobles whom they named, as well as certain clerics whom they did not name of the dioceses of Ossory and Leighlin, 'more cruel than Pharaoh ... do not fear to subjugate the said monastery to their jurisdiction and temporal rule as if it were their own patrimony, compel the abbot and convent ... to give and pay them feudal dues, stipends, tallages, commons, private subsidies, collections, protection money, compel the men and subjects thereof to wars at their own expense and to give and pay fines and many other penalties, exactions and servitudes which they have been wont to exact and receive from their own lay subjects, and to undergo all other lay burdens, and otherwise fear not to afflict the said monastery and its subjects with divers taxations and to impose the same upon them by reason of [3] which things all the buildings of the monastery are threatened with ruin'.

Whether conditions as a result of this plea improved or not is not known, but it is interesting to note that Donald MacMurrogh, Lord of all Leinster 'granted 8d from every ploughland in his dominion to this abbey 1475'.[4] What prompted the gesture is not known, but in November of that year excessive flooding by the River Barrow inundated the Abbot's garden and the floor of the infirmary Chapel. In 1501 Charles O'Kavanagh was appointed Abbot. This man seems to have tried to put the Abbey back in good order and was 'ever zealous for the well-being of our house'. He enriched the church with many costly presents, among them a magnificent chased silver cross decorated with gems, a cope, a chasuble and two tunics. He was apparently a capable man. In 1516 he was appointed Vicar General to the Bishop of Leighlin and when

he was away from the Abbey in this capacity, Prior Nicholas looked after the monastery.

The large Chalice is the Kavanagh Chalice. The smaller is a Butler Chalice. In the centre the Casey Silver Cross.

All was not well, however. In 1501 Henry VII arranged a marriage between his elder son Arthur and Catherine of Aragon. Arthur died and in order to retain the Spanish Alliance Henry VII proposed to marry his second son (the future Henry VIII) to Arthur's widow. The law of the Church forbade a man to marry his deceased brother's wife, so a dispensation was asked for and obtained from Julius II and in 1509 Henry VIII married Catherine of Aragon just after his accession to the throne. They were married for twenty years and had six children only one of whom lived, a daughter named Mary. Henry became worried that he had no male heir to succeed him, so he decided to divorce Catherine and marry Ann Boleyn. In 1527 Henry asked the new Pope, Clement VII, to declare that the dispensation which had been given to him by Julius II was incorrect and should not have been granted. After long consideration Pope Clement VII upheld the decision of Julius II. This began the quarrel between Henry VIII and the Papacy. In 1529 he broke with Rome and made himself Supreme Head of the Church and Clergy of England. In 1532 he still hoped to force Clement VII to give him his dispensation by the Act of Annates whereby he threatened to take for himself the first year's revenues which newly appointed bishops and abbots paid to the Pope. We know for certain that he took the tenths belonging to St Mary's Abbey, Dublin,[5] but the Pope ignored the Act and Henry VIII was excommunicated.

Henry's reply to his excommunication was to pass the Act of Supremacy by which he became 'only Supreme Head on earth of the Church of England'. Henry knew very well that there was one branch of the Church which he could not be sure of controlling and that was the monasteries. The monasteries had a special place, for they were not controlled by the bishops in whose diocese they were, but owed their obedience to their own superiors or to visitors appointed by the Pope. Henry was also attracted to the abbeys by their great wealth but his pretext for suppressing them was different. In 1534 he passed an Act of Supremacy which gave him authority to visit all institutions of the Church in order to search out and correct abuses. In 1535 he appointed Thomas Cromwell his vicar general to report on conditions in the monasteries. Cromwell and his agents knew what was expected of them and in their reports on the English houses they painted a terrifying picture of ignorance, sloth and immorality. In the Irish Houses the only charge against the monks was that they were addicted to the pestiferous doctrines of the Roman Pontiff.[6]

In 1530 Abbot Kavanagh had taken ague (rheumatism or arthritis). His doctor Kairwaun Daly, advised him that it was caused by the damp climate of Ireland. The Abbot then decided to go to Germany to St James' Ratisbon to see if the dryness of that country would improve his condition. As a result of this, contact was made with the German Abbey. As deputy Vicar General to the Bishop of Leighlin, Abbot Kavanagh knew what was happening to the monasteries in England and he knew that a similar fate was in store for the Irish monasteries. In 1536 an Act of Suppression to dissolve the lesser monasteries was introduced.

The question now arose as to what exactly a lesser monastery was and this was settled according to population and income. Any monastery with more than twelve inhabitants was large; any monastery with more than £200 of an income was great and these were not suppressed. However there were many, many monasteries with fewer than twelve monks, but more than £200 income and vice versa. So the criterion actually used was that based on income: any monastery with less than £200 was suppressed. Of twelve monasteries in Ireland immediately dissolved, five were Cistercian: Baltinglass, Bective, Duiske, Dunbrody and Tintern, all of which were situated within the Pale, or the Anglo-Irish Lordship.

Before the Dissolution, Abbot Kavanagh leased part of the abbey lands to his kinsmen. He sent some of the older monks to the exempted monasteries and he sent some of the younger monks to St

James' Ratisbon; some however did not leave Duiske Abbey.

In a very early Charter of the Abbey of Duiske, there is a curious condition made by Adam Fitz-sinnot where he claims the privilege for himself and his heirs for ever of presenting one monk who can speak English to the Abbey of Duiske. So it must have appeared to Adam that the Irish would eventually predominate in Duiske. 'Predicti vero monachi concessurunt michi recepturos se monachum unum ad presentationem meam... qui tamem de lingua Anglica sit...' [7]

This prediction did not come true. The Abbey was soon to be dissolved; some of its possessions were already scattered. In 1531 Chief Baron of the Exchequer, Patrick Finglas, recommended that 'divers abbeys adjoining to these Irishmen which give more aid to them than to the King, such as the Abbey of Duiske may be suppressed and given to young lords and gentlemen of England who shall dwell upon the same'. [8]

On 4 January 1541 an extent of the abbey property was made at Kilkenny in the presence of Abbot Kavanagh and Hugh Smith, Darby Finns, Edward Butler, Nicholas Fitz Power, Thomas Conner, William Ryan, William Fitzdaly and Donald Fitzpower. The Abbot received the grange of Killenny for sixty-one years and a pension of £10.00. [9] No other monk received a pension. The lands were transferred to the Crown, but the King gave a lease of the estate to J. Butler grand nephew of the Abbot for twenty-one years and this became the Manor of Duiske. [10] Between 1541-1697 the lands were held by eight generations of Butlers. In 1546 the estate passed to the fifth son of James

Butler Castle at Graignamanagh. (Above)

Butler Coat of Arms, Duiske Abbey. (Right)

Butler, also called James.[11] In 1559 this man petitioned the Queen for the renewing of the lease of the abbey which had been given to his father twenty-one years before and this was granted on 26 January 1561,[12] the only reservation being that 'the buildings were to be maintained and that the lands were not be set to any persons, not English by both parents'.

The Butlers did not reside in the abbey. The nearest Butler residence to Duiske Abbey was at Tinnahinch Castle, built around this time to protect the ford across the River Barrow to Duiske Abbey. This castle is still standing, a massive square foundation on a rock outcrop. The entrance was on the west side and was defended by a bartizan at the top of the building. The north and east sides were defended by a turret. At a later period this castle was strengthened, original windows were built up and port holes bored through the original walls in many places. Thus as far as Duiske Abbey is concerned the Butlers had Killenny and Tinnahinch Castle. James Butler was not content with the lease which he got in 1561 and in 1566 he petitioned the Crown for a fee farm of the abbey lands.[13]

The petition was granted and letters patent were issued. Why James Butler was not content with the lease and his desire for the grant under letters patent suggests that he wished for more firm control, if not outright possession of the Abbey. As already mentioned only the Abbot received a pension and it is probable that the monks remained in Duiske Abbey. As already stated James Butler lived in Tinnahinch Castle, his grand uncle the Abbot lived in Killenny, all were Catholics and it is hardly likely that the monks were turned out. Tradition has it that twelve monks who resisted the Elizabethan forces were slain at a place near the Abbey Church called the Black Bout. It is remarkable too that the lease issued under letters patent substitutes

This area is known as the Black Bout, the place where the Twelve Monks were murdered.

'curates to be maintained in the churches, on the property' instead of 'the buildings were to be maintained'. 'Buildings to be maintained' could only be maintained through habitation by monks, 'curates to be maintained in the churches on the property' only required a priest in the Abbey Church, and in the churches of Annamult, Tullachany, Ballyle, Kylcombre. Perhaps the second lay owner was horrified at the treatment of the monks and was concerned that Catholicism might no longer be practised in Duiske, whereupon he received the lands under letters patent and had a clause inserted that priests were to serve in the Churches. James Butler died soon afterwards and in 1567 a grant was made to his son, also named James Butler.[14] This James Butler had no heir and the Abbey lands reverted to his uncle Thomas, tenth Earl of Ormonde, who conveyed them in 1579 to his illegitimate son

Piers Butler.[15] The latter died in 1601 and was succeeded by his son Sir Edward Butler, who became Viscount Galmoy in 1646.[16] The Abbey estates remained in the family of Sir Edward Butler until 1697 when they were forfeited, as the third Viscount Galmoy took the side of James II in the Williamite wars.[17] In 1703 the confiscated abbey lands were sold and were purchased by James Agar of Gowran and from that they passed to the Clifden family.[18]

Indeed in the same year the Dublin Parliament decided that the Barrow was a trade route that must be developed at all public cost. That accelerated the growth of the modern town. By 1765 some three miles of shallow had been made navigable. By 1790, sixty barges could moor along the quays. In 1802 it was a fair sized town and according to Tighe's Statistical Survey it had three hundred and seventy houses. The Abbey must have completely disappeared underneath the village. In 1809 the Abbey Church and portions of its ruins had been granted in perpetuity to the Catholics twenty years before Catholic emancipation. To P. O'Leary we must leave the last trace of the monk's village — Graignamanagh. The latter has traced their encroachment as follows:-

1. Mrs. T. Byrne Grocer, Stationer, Restaurant.
2. Archway.
3. Garda Barracks.
4. Late Patrick O'Leary — now E.A. Hughes, Bakery, Flour Stores and yard Hughes with Archway.
5. John M. Murphy & Son Gen. Merch. Shop, Yard and Stores.
6. Thom. Joyce Public House and Provisions.
7. P. O'Leary Bakery, confectioner stat. newsagent.
8a. J. O'Leary Bakery, stores yard.
8b. Frank Murray Draper, yard stores shed.

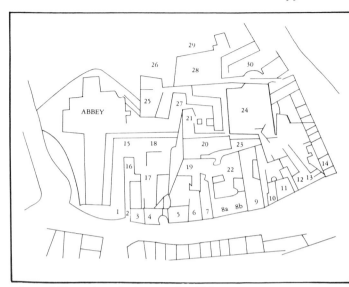

Map of Town in relation to the Abbey.

9. T. Joyce, Draper & Furniture, Shop, Stores and Yard.
   Lane between 9-10. Under the street surface here, are the remains of the Curia or boundary wall of the Abbey enclosure.
10. Miss M. Lennon, Grocery, Shop, Provisions.
11. T. Joyce, Furniture Shop, Shop & Yard.
12. Wm. Shea Publican Shop, Yard & Garden.
13. Wm. Shea and Garda Cregan Shop residence and yard.
14. Martin Hennessey Draper & Publican, Shop & Yard.
15. Late P. O'Leary now E.A. Hughes.
    The corner here is now the Baptistry of Parish Abbey Church with processional Door/Site of North Walk of cloister, middle part stables & lofts.
    West end. Mrs. T. Byrne's no 1 premises
    East corner Baptistry.
16. Late P. O'Leary now E.A. Hughes open yard.

17. Late P. O'Leary now E.A. Hughes Site of W. cloister walk.
19. J.M. Murphy & Son Hardware Stores.
20. John Prendergast. Corn Store.
21. J.P. Hughes. Store lofts.
22. F. Murray. Draper.
23. F. Murray & Thos. Joyce space divided between these two.
    J. Joyces is now a furniture store.
24 Late P. O'Leary now E.A. Hughes.
    East boundary walls here represents the remains of the Abbey. Infirmary buildings with windows & fire places.
25. Part of precinct of Parish Abbey Church.
    Site of enlarged Chapter House and Scriptorium of Duiske.
26. Do. Recently added portion of Parish Cemetery.
27. J.P. Hughes.
    Ancient site of monks' cemetery.
28. M.J. O'Connell Garden.
    Probably a curve in the river bank in the monastic period and under water.
29. Do. Yards and sheds.
30. Late P. O'Leary now E.A. Hughes yards and sheds.
    Do. Infirmary windows looked out on this space.

A Town Remembers

Duiske Abbey Church in 1889 drawn by John O'Leary. Note the thatched Penal Mass House.

The Butlers continued to provide for Catholic priests in Graignamanagh. In the liber Regalis Visitations of 4 July 1615 mention is made that in 'Monasterium de Duiske alias Graige: Edwardus Butler qui ibidem retinet sacerdotem papesticum' and the Rev. John Brennan was chaplain to him in Killenny and Richard Marub was chaplain to James Butler of Tinnachinch Castle and he also supported another priest called Fr Mathew Roche. During the Penal times a Mass House was erected within the abbey. The altar could be seen from the window of the treasury. Today the same Penal Altar is still extant. One of the side chapels of Duiske Abbey is used as a vestry for priests, the other was given to the Sisters of Mercy when they came to Graignamanagh in 1900 and it is this side chapel that the nuns use.

In 1754 part of the west end of Duiske Abbey was roofed in by Parson Owens but was never used by the Protestant Community. However, in 1810 Rector Alcock and his committee decided to move to a new site and they built a church called St

Peter's. To help their building project they took the roof from the west end with them but did not take the bell. With the rapid growth of the Barrow navigation system Graignamanagh expanded. The Penal mass house was no longer adequate for the people. The former monastic lands were in the hands of three men, Agar, Clifden and Annaly. On 1 February 1812 Viscount Clifden decided to give the Abbey Church to the Catholic Community. A panel of twenty-three trustees from different parts of the United Parishes of Graige and Ullard was drawn up and an indenture was made between the Right Honorable Henry Welbore, Lord Viscount Clifden and these twenty-three parishioners. The names of the twenty-three were Timothy Doyle, William Cheevers, James Murphy, William Flaherty, John Kenny, James Cawey, Thomas Clooney, Ignatius Rossiter, Thomas Murphy and Michael Murphy all of Graige and Darby Byrne, John Byrne and Luke Flaherty of Ullard, John Byrne of Barnwarden, Bernard Farrell and Patrick Farrell of Brandon Park, Robert Doyle of Graige, John Doyle of Aclare, Michael Mahon of Coolroe, James Doyle, Denis Doyle, William Joyce and Edward Joyce all of Ballyogan (witnesses). The indenture states that 'for and in consideration of the Loyalty and good conduct of the Roman Catholic inhabitants of the Parish of Graige aforesaid the said Viscount desires to provide them with a suitable place for the performance of Divine Worship.'[1]

The people of Graige and Ullard were given the Ancient Abbey of Graige comprising the Choir, North and South transepts and the nave, independent of the side Aisles, part of which, namely the Nave had been formerly used as a Protestant Church 'which said premises extend from east to west two hundred and seven feet five inches and from north to south one hundred and fourteen feet one inch'.[2] The Rev. Lewis Moore was Parish Priest

Duiske Abbey, Graignamanagh, in 1927. Notice the Barber's pole, the cobbled roadside and the window bars for displaying goods for sale.

and the people were required to pay ten shillings yearly for the church. This payment was to be in two instalments, five shillings in May and five shillings in November. The indenture also stated that if any of the twenty-three trustees mentioned above died then the Parish Priest had to notify Viscount Clifden and his heirs to appoint another trustee. If within twelve calendar months Viscount Clifden did not do this then the Parish Priest should convene a meeting of the surviving trustees, allowing ten days notice for the meeting. At that meeting the Trustees should nominate an inhabitant of the United Parishes of Graige and Ullard to replace the deceased member. The indenture was signed, sealed and delivered by Lord Visct. Clifden, E. Woodnutt, Francis Barrett, Tho. Nowlan and by the aforementioned twenty-three trustees.[3]

This agreement released Viscount Clifden from having to maintain the buildings, for it was now the responsibility of the people of Graige. The parishioners decided that the first necessity was to put a new roof on the Abbey. A man called Robinson prepared plans and scale drawings for the project. Such a restoration would have cost £5,000 and he offered to supervise the restoration free of charge provided that the parish would allow him to restore it completely in character with its medieval origin. Unfortunately the Parish could not raise such a vast sum and the work was mainly devoted to re-roofing the abbey. The Parish united in its effort, giving whatever help they could. In fact it is told that a woman who had nothing to offer in the way of money offered to 'pull the grass to feed the horses at dinner time'. These were the farmers' horses that brought loads of stone and mortar to the abbey.

The population of Graignamanagh as a river side settlement with navigation interests continued to grow. Hitherto all the five to six ton boats built in Graignamanagh known as Clarahawns were hauled by teams of eight men pulling the boat with ropes, four being positioned on either bank. If any of the Clarahawns did not pull to match the strength of the other members of the team, then the boat slewed and he was nicknamed 'Hollowback'.

After 1750 with the making of the Dry dock at Graignamanagh the population continued to increase. From the navigation system two organisations emerged, the Barrow Anchor Society and the Guild of Boatmen. These were the people who concerned themselves with re-roofing the Abbey. This was a low pitched roof, local flags were obtained from Flag Mount Slate quarries and kitchen flags for flooring near Paulstown.

Cross at Duiske Abbey.

The people were excited they had been given a church 207 feet 5 inches from east to west, from the alter to the back of the church and 114 feet 1 inch from north to south.[4] Splendid but staggering to people who had never had seating accommodation in church and they wondered how they would see the altar from such a distance.

The answer lay in the erection of galleries. The Guild of Tradesmen sat in the north transept, the Boatmen sat in the south transept and the business men and farmers sat in the nave of the church. Each family had its own seats, and each group formed a benevolent society. On the death of a member, the family of the deceased received £3 towards funeral expenses. The members of the Guild had to meet the funeral cortege of a deceased member three miles out from the Abbey, clean and neatly dressed, wearing a white sash.

After the re-roofing of 1813 secular burials continued within the church, the west end that had been occupied by Protestants was roofed in 1887 and between 1850-1900 a new wooden floor and tiling was completed. For close on fifty years from 1875 to 1925 embellishment of the Abbey Church took place. After the re-roofing of the west end of the Church in 1887, the people of Graignamanagh decided that they would like a new bell. The Abbey bells had been sold to the Duke of Ormond in 1541[5] and the existing bell was made by Sheridan of Dublin in 1844. To house this bell, a campanula had been built. Fr McDonnel arranged for this bell to be taken down and erected outside the church, When it was rung at this level it had a beautiful tone, but not when in the campanula. The people however wanted a tuneful bell. They were anxious to have a bell made in an Irish Foundry, but this could not be obtained so Patrick and John O'Leary went to London to a company called Warner Bros whose warehouse was near Cricklegate. They exp-

lained to Warners how much money they had to spend and were shown a tenor bell, the St Giles Bell, weighing eighteen cwts and costing £5 per cwt. This bell was guaranteed by the firm and was purchased and brought by boat to the quay side at Tinnahinch. Then it was brought through the town on a boggey. The people of Graignamanagh hauled it up the street and it was taken into the church on a trolley and then hoisted one-hundred and fifty feet to its present position. No mean feat considering the lack of space in the campanula. The town remembers the day the occupants of High Street came out of their homes onto the roadway when it was struck and its magnificent tone reverberated over the valley. The people were elated. Every Sunday at 10 o'clock the bell for sacred reading was rung and at 11 o'clock the bell rang again and the choir assembled before the altar. The old bell was given to the Franciscan Friary of Mt Bellew in Galway by Fr McDonnell.

About this time also it was decided to undertake painting of the interior. The services of some peripatetic Italian artists were obtained and the themes chosen were the Ascension of Our Lord and the Assumption of Our Lady. On the four corners of the flat ceiling of the Choir there were paintings depicting the Four Evangelists; Matthew, Mark, Luke and John. The design in the centre crossing was a Saint Catherine's wheel and it was hoped this would give the impression of a dome. Biblical quotations were painted in ornate lettering on the frieze at ceiling level around the perimeter of the Church. Perhaps at a later date all this was thought to be a distraction to Divine Service or perhaps the concentration of paintings in the Choir left other parts of the Church unattractive. Whatever the reason the colourful Italian designs and Biblical quotations were painted over in 1928/29 when the Church was again re-decorated. Embellishment of

Interior Paintings c 1887-1929

the abbey increased, stained glass windows were inserted, the East Window by Patrick and Christopher Hughes, in memory of the Rev James Hughes, Dean of Maynooth. This is a much admired window and has been described as 'an excellent window of the period, colourful and lets in the light'. It is thought that the two smaller windows over the side chapels in the north and south transepts were given to the church by Fr McDonnell. There are two other stained glass windows of the rich dark type of glass, inserted between 1925-30; one is the Ryan window and the other is the Mulligan window. Of the remaining windows all had new frames and glass inserted after internal and external plastering was done in 1950.

The Abbey Church needed to be railed off, and around 1880 Patrick O'Leary designed the railings, the timber moulds for the railings were made by Billy Walsh, the iron castings were made locally by Jas B Walsh of the foundry and the iron work was done by Patrick Hammond.

In 1954 the Eire Government inaugurated a scheme called 'An Tostal' — 'bring our exiles home', and have a celebration for them. Many generations of exiles had been baptised in Duiske Abbey. The Year 1954 coincided with the 750th anniversary of the founding of the Abbey. A grant was received from Bord Failte to clean up the disused Chapter house, to remove the thirteenth century effigy of Alan Beg to within the Abbey, to clean up the ninth century Celtic Ackyltaun, and to erect a protective railing on the 13th century Castle of Coolhill, the former home of De La Roche the disappointed lover of Eilleen Aroon and descriptive plates were put on Tinnahinch Castle and Duiske Abbey. Big efforts were being made to mark the commemoration. Permission was sought from the Bishop, Dr Keough, to mark the event by asking the monks of Mt Mellerey Abbey to return to Duiske Abbey and celebrate mass with plain Chant Singing. The Abbot Dom Celsus O'Connel was enthusiastic and agreed, plans were prepared to accord the monks a suitable reception and a souvenir publication was planned. It was also hoped to have the Bishops of Ferns, Ossory and Leighlin present, in an effort to repeat the religious services which according to the Charters took place on the 6 June 1204. Alas the celebration did not take place; Dom Celsus O'Connel wrote to say that he could not attend as he had to go to the opening of a new daughter house Our Lady of the Southern Star in New Zealand.

In 1962 Fr William Gavin was appointed Parish Priest and soon afterwards told the parishioners that the Diocesan Architects had examined the roof and the structure and concluded that major repairs were necessary, if not a total new roof. In 1963 a fund was opened to commemorate the tercentenary of the first restoration project of 1813 when the Abbey was raised to Parish Status.

The work on Ballintubber Abbey and Holy Cross Abbey accelerated and highlighted the idea of restoration of Medieval monastic foundations. At this time the late Fr Killian OCSO, Mount Mellerey Abbey, Co Waterford wrote an article 'Abbey in Crisis', which was published in the *Munster Express* about Duiske Abbey. Fr Athanasius O'Brien OCSO took a photograph of a dormitory window of Duiske Abbey to illustrate it. Fr Killian sent a copy of that booklet to me and I felt that some day I would visit Duiske Abbey. The publication of 'Abbey in Crisis', was followed by talks given by Mr Percy le Clerc, Dr S O'Faolain and the Kilkenny Archaeological Society who all helped to focus attention on the question of whether the condition of the church was such as would justify the major outlay on work in character with the fabric of the Abbey or should the Abbey be vacated and a new church erected. At this time a Parish council had been formed. However because of its location in the centre of the town, and the affiliation of the parish church with the Medieval Church, the Parish Council decided that any outlay or expense should be expended on the preservation of the existing Abbey Church. The parishioners then by plebiscite likewise decided that any outlay or expense should be expended on the preservation in character of the historic Abbey and Parish Church. In their wisdom the Parish Council decided to recommend to the Parish the principle that whatever money was to be spent was to be on the Abbey and not on a new Church. With this recommendation the Parish by plebiscite decided to remain in the Abbey and plans were accordingly prepared. The question now arose, were the people of Graige anxious for restoration or renovation and it was clearly decided that any money lavished on the Medieval Church was to be in character with the ancient fabric of Duiske Abbey.

Having heard of the Parish decision the Bishop gave the project his blessing and the work was commenced in March 1974.

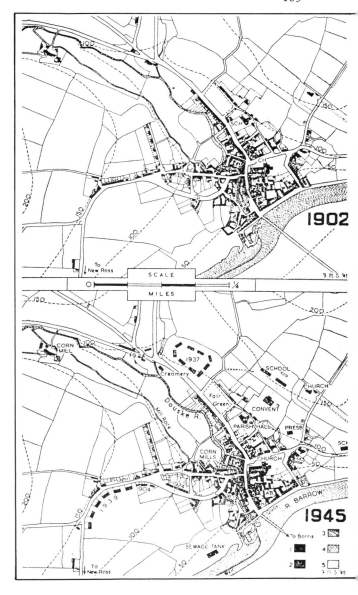

The Town of Graiguenamanagh, 1902 and 1945.
1902, all buildings in solid black; 1945, key, 1, Public building, including shops; 2, Substantial houses; 3, Cottage type houses; 4, Vacant buildings; 5, Barns and sheds.
Note that the town has spread outwards and has become less congested.
Based on the Ordnance Survey, 25 ins. to one mile, 1902, by permission of the Minister for Finance of Ireland. 1945 observations by Social Group, Field Study week, 1945; map drawn by F. M. Synge.

Epilogue

The story goes that in 1812 a man named O'Leary lived in Clonegal near the Carlow Wexford border. He eloped with Kitty Anderson the miller's daughter and came to Graignamanagh. He was a baker, a bacon curer and a business man. At this time the people of Graignamanagh brought their dough for bread making to the local public oven to be baked. The person in charge of the oven took a piece of everybody's dough in return for the use of the oven. All these pieces were baked together and the quality and texture of these when baked was known as 'Linsey Woolsey (linseed) Bread'. This was then sold to the public by the community bakers. The latter were all women. The last of the community ovens is in a cellar under O'Shea's Bar in High Street — a relic of the social history of those days.

This man started his own business first at Tinnahinch, later at Lower Main Street and finally settled in the shadow of the Abbey/Refectory using one of its walls as the main support for his bakehouse. This couple had two sons, James O'Leary and Edward O'Leary and one daughter Anastasia. James married Elizabeth Bray and moved further up the street where he erected his bakehouse in the Cloister garth. It was Edward O'Leary who later first began to investigate the plan and buildings of Duiske Abbey, in this he was helped by his fellow townsman, friend and contemporary, Reverend James Hughes, Dean of Maynooth who sent him a text by Bloxham (an authority on Medieval Church Architecture) and with the aid of this he sketched the outline and unfolded the Abbey plan from under the great mass of 19th century building into which they had been converted. He was an Artist of considerable ability and his sketches later illustrated Rev M Comerford's 'Account of the Parishes of Graignamanagh and St Mullins'. Edward O'Leary had nine children, six boys and three girls, five of whom died young. John was the only surviving boy and Kate and Nessie two sisters. John took over the business when his father became ill. He began work as a baker at twelve years of age and had an artistic gift in cake decoration. He specialised in wedding cakes which were sent all over the world, which had Celtic Motifs on them. At this time there were itinerant bakers, who would work on Friday and Saturday and leave on Monday, whom he sometimes engaged. Edward O'Leary decided to get somebody permanent but found it hard to find a suitable person. However one day he interviewed a man named Tom Roche. He asked Tom how good he was. Tom replied, 'Every day I gets up and I stands at the tro' (trough) I learn something new'. Edward O'Leary employed him and he was the best baker he ever had and he stayed with him until he died. Like his father before him John also was an artist and collaborated with his cousins Patrick and William in compiling the booklet 'Graignamanagh Abbey'. His black and white illustrations, particularly of the Abbey before its suppression and other aspects of monastic life would do credit to many a professional. John died in 1963 having been successively honoured as President of the Kilkenny Archaeological Society of which he was a founder member.

James had six children, one of whom was called Patrick. Like his father Patrick became a baker by trade, but in his spare time he helped to keep interest in the abbey alive. He also had a salt works, a lime kiln supplying lime to farmers, and culm which was Castlecomer anthracite, all of which was sold to farmers on the Fair Days.

In his spare time he excavated St Mullins and found the round tower there. Then he wrote the booklet on St Mullin's. He was also entrusted with the contract work on Carigglade Hill, lowering it by twelve feet at the top and filling it in at the bottom which made it easier for people to come into Graignamanagh. He supervised the re-building of Borris Church, the Parish Priests' house, the Convent of Mercy, the creamery, the teachers' residence, and the sack store. His available spare time he spent in and around the Abbey Church: he designed the newel post for the stairway to the baptistry, the railings, and swung the new bell; he supervised the re-building of the priests' vestry but his greatest love was for music, particularly Irish music and to any itinerant musician it was Cead Mile Failte.

Patrick, William and John and two brothers who were bootmakers called Bernard and Mike Fenon and a singer called James O'Donnel used to have Sunday concerts over the bakery. As they played the people assembled in the street to enjoy the concert. He also organised and looked after the band in Graignamanagh and wrote about 'The Old Bands'. He was very interested in boating, and the revival of the regatta. He wrote 'Half-hours with the Old Boatmen', which is really an account of the Barrow navigation system.

In 1915 when the Vatican wished to record the names of all those who were martyred in the Penal times, evidence was collected in various districts including Graignamanagh. In this connection Abbot Stanislaus of Mount Mellerey came to collect evidence in Graignamanagh and visited Patrick O'Leary. Patrick showed the Abbot the place where the twelve monks of Duiske were murdered, a place still called the 'Black Bout'. Then together they visited older citizens of Graignamanagh and the Abbot was convinced that a mass murder did take place. An ecclesiastical inquiry was held in Clonliffe College in 1915 and the person who presented the case was Patrick O'Leary. At the end of the hearing a decree was issued:-

DECREE
DIOCESE OF DUBLIN

Introduction of the Cause of the Beatification or Declaration of Martyrdom of the Servants of God:-

DERMOT O'HURLEY
Archbishop of Cashel
CORNELIUS O'DEVANY Order of St. Francis
Bishop of Down and Connor
TERENCE ABBOT O'BRIEN Order of Preachers
Bishop of Emly
AND COMPANIONS

In Ireland, nurse of heroes during the ruthless and savage persecutions against Catholics which broke out in the Sixteenth and Seventeenth Centuries there were put to death innumerable champions of Christ whose names unknown to mortals are written in the Book of Life, of many others the names and fame still live in the memory of men.

N.B. the case accepted referred to 'Two Hundred

and Fifty Seven Servants of God'.

Included were:-

OF THE CISTERCIAN ORDER: Gelasius O'Cullenan, Nicholas Fitzgerald, *The Prior and Monks of the Abbey of St. Saviour*, Patrick O'Connor, Malachy O'Kelly, The Abbot and Monks of the Abbey of Manister, Eugene O'Gallagher, Bernard O'Treivir, James Eustace, Malachy Sheil, Edmund Mulligan, Luke Bergin.

The case of twenty three Servants of God was postponed awaiting the production of Stronger Proofs.

The 9th day of February, 1915

(Seal)   Anthony, Lord Vico, S.R.C. Pro Prefect

+ Peter La Fontaine, Bishop of Carystos

Secretary.

Tablet in memory of the 'Man in the Cloisters'.

This was Patrick O'Leary's finest achievement. This short biographical sketch is inadequate as a portrait of Patrick O'Leary, his life, his work. Such a task must be undertaken by a professional biographer.

Patrick O'Leary as a young man was strong, athletic, about five feet eight inches and slightly built. His contributions to the everyday life of the people and commemorative occasions is inestimable. This is recognised by all. When Fr Murphy, a Parish Priest of Borris and a life long friend, asked Bishop Keough's permission to erect a plaque on the walls of Duiske Abbey, the Bishop said 'Nobody deserves it better than he. Put it either inside or outside.' This inscription was composed by Fr Murphy and the slab was prepared by Brennan of the Royal Oak Bagnalstown.

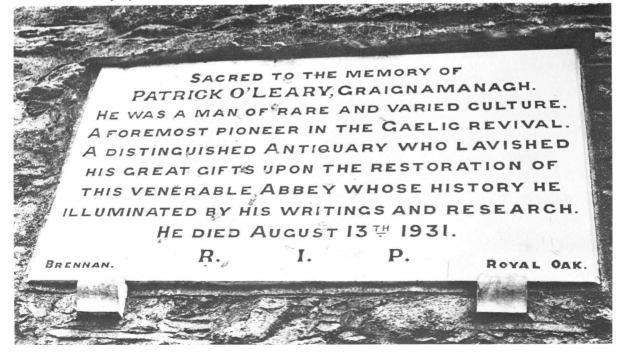

Appendix A

PASTORS OF GRAIGNAMANAGH

Compiled by an t-Atair Peadar MacSuibne, P.P. Cilldara from Comerford. Collections I, II, III, Irish Catholic Directory and Knockbeg Centenary Book.

In 1618 according to an old return, the P.P. was Fr. John Brennan who 'keepeth from the most part with Mr. Edward Butler of the Old Abbey, gentleman'.

In 1704, Fr. Anthony Forstall was P.P. He lived at Pollagh and was aged 48. He was ordained in Spain in 1676 and his sureties were William Butler, Bramblestown and Charles Purcell, Cloghlea.

In 1731, Fr. Robert Rossiter was P.P. He died in February 1769 and is buried at St. Mullins.

In 1766, Fr. Denis O'Connor P.P. Borris had charge of the district of Ullard.

In 1769, on the death of Fr. Rossiter, Fr. Laurence Clooney became P.P. He died on the 10 October 1796, but he appears to have resigned or retired from the administration of the parish several years before that. He is buried at St. Mullins.

About 1770, Fr. Henry Staunton, then recently ordained, came as administrator to Graignamanagh, where later he became P.P. In 1798, Fr. Staunton became Dean of the Chapter of Leighlin. In March 1787, he left Graignamanagh to become P.P. of Carlow and first President of Carlow College which opened in October 1793. He died 1 September 1814. He was a native of Kellymount.

Dean Staunton was succeeded as P.P. Graignamanagh by Fr. R. Fitzgerald. He died 6 July 1805, and is interred in the Abbey Church.

Fr. Fitzgerald was succeeded by Fr. Lewis Moore who was translated from Borris where he had been P.P. since 1799. He died June 1818 and is buried in the Abbey Church.

Fr. Moore was succeeded by Fr. Benjamin Joseph Branghall, a native of Kildare town. Soon after his ordination in 1807, he became C.C. in Raheen and directed the building of the Chapel-of-Ease at Shanahoe. In 1821, he obtained leave of absence from the bishop, Dr. Doyle, to go on a pilgrimage to the Holy Land. During his absence, the parish was administered by Fr. Maurice Kearney, a native of Lorum, who became P.P. of Clane in 1824, and subsequently by Fr. Patrick Kehoe, a native of Carrick in Dunleckney parish and brother of Fr. Michael Kehoe P.P. Abbeyleix. Fr. P. Kehoe became P.P. Leighlin probably about May 1829, succeeding Fr. James Maher who became P.P. Paulstown.

In 1827, Fr. Branghall resigned the parish and was succeeded by Fr. Martin Doyle who had previously been P.P. Clonegal, where he had erected the parish church. In 1839 Fr. Branghall went as a pilgrim to Rome and to Italy. He was admitted into the Benedictine Monastery of Monte Cassino in 1840, where he died in 1850 with a great reputation for sanctity. A small residence which Fr. Branghall built for himself in his early career as P.P. still stands. His chair, donated by the late Fr. Patrick Gorry P.P. Monasterevan who died 18 September 1958 is preserved at the Mercy Convent.

His successor Fr. Martin Doyle was a native of Ballinvegga, near New Ross, and a first cousin of J.K.L. Under the guidance of J.K.L. he was leader in the anti-tithe war. He died 4 August 1861 and is buried in the Abbey Church.

Fr. Denis Flanagan succeeded. He was transferred as P.P. to Suncroft in December 1868.

Fr. Bernard O'Neill was the next P.P. He was a native of Ballyoliver in Rathvilly parish. He was Adm. Carlow 1865-69. In October 1881, he was transferred as P.P. to Bagnelstown where he died 27 January 1892.

He was succeeded in Graignamanagh by Fr. Patrick McDonnell, who had previously been P.P. of Hacketstown. He was born in Mullaghanard, Rosenallis parish. He died 18 March 1901.

Mr. Joseph Mooney, a native of Quarrymount in Mountmellick parish and brother of Fr. John Mooney P.P. Clonegal was the next P.P. He died 11 June 1925.

He was succeeded by Fr. Thomas Dowling who was translated from Myshall. He was a native of Kylegrove, Ballyfin. He died 9 March 1934.

The next P.P. was Fr. Patrick Donnelly B.A. a native of Rathvilly parish. He died 16 February 1937.

He was succeeded by Fr. Patrick Hayden B.A. He was a native of Rathanna parish of Borris. He died 13 June 1956.

He was succeeded by Fr. Thomas Donohoe. 1956-64.

Present Parish Priest is Fr. William Gavin.

Appendix B

CURATES OF GRAIGNAMANAGH

In 1766, Fr. Laurence Clooney was Assistant, that is curate to Fr. Rossiter P.P. From his epitaph at St. Mullins it is probable that he had been curate from 1747, and possibly before that. He became P.P. Graignamanagh in 1769. He died in 1796 aged 96.

According to Dr. Doyle's list of Diocesan Clergy of 1820 'Rev Mr. Nowlan of Leighlin' was curate of Graigue in that year and had been appointed in 1815. Leighlin was his native parish and at that time included portion of the present parish of Paulstown. This Fr. Nowlan C.C. may be 'Master Michael Nowlan of Co. Kilkenny' who was a Carlow College student from 1809 until 1 July 1816. Dr. Doyle's 1815 may have been an error for 1816.

In 1830, a Fr. Nolan C.C. left the parish to see a dying kinsman, and when that fact was brought to J.K.L.'s notice by the P.P. Fr. Martin Doyle, the bishop wrote: 'Mr. Nolan is only lingering from hour to hour, and it is hard to send away from him his only near friend, but I will say what you wish to your curate, and if the danger be not imminent, I am sure he will return: if it be I think you would not wish him home.'

In January of that year J.K.L. had asked Fr. Martin Doyle P.P. to be his agent with the priests of St. Mullins and with his own C.C. Fr. Nolan in the meritorious cause of the new Cathedral.

According to the same Diocesan Clergy list of 1820, 'Rev. Fr. Prendergast of Leighlin' was C.C. Graigue, and had been appointed in 1818. As we have seen, Leighlin parish at this time included part of the present parish of Paulstown. He may be 'Martin Prendergast of Paulstown' who was a student of Carlow College from 1808 until July 1816. On J.K.L.'s list is a note written at a later date 'Of Connoght' (sic) See if Chaplain to the Reddingtons. In Paulstown Churchyard there is a stone 'erected by John Prendergast to ... his uncle, Rev. Martin Prendergast who died 19 March 1864 at Kilcorman Castle, Co. Galway, where he had been chaplain to Sir Thomas Redington and his family for 40 years'.

The following names and dates are taken from the Catholic Registry, which was first published in 1836, and from the Irish Catholic Directory which succeeded it. The month of coming to, and leaving Graignamanagh can in many if not in most cases be ascertained from the entries in the baptismal and other registers of the parish.

1835 — '39	Fr. Michael Nolan is C.C. He is doubtless Fr. Michael Nolan who became P.P. Myshall in January 1839. He died in 1852 aged 60. He is buried in Holy Cross Church Myshall near the Eleventh Station. According to a tradition in Myshall he was a native of that parish. Vid Comerford III. 172. 320. *Knockbeg Centenary Book* pp 56, 83.
1835 — '48	Patrick Doyle, possibly Fr. Patrick Doyle a native of Ballyling, and P.P. Philipstown 1850: nephew Fr. Martin, died 20 October 1866.
1849	James Doyle, possibly an error for Patrick Doyle.
1840	N. Dunne. Probably Fr. Mathew Dunne.
1841 — '43	Mathew Dunne. Possibly Rev. M. Dunne, Kildare and Leighlin who died in 1867.
1844	James Hayd'n. A native of Carlow and son of Dr. Hayden, physician to Carlow College. He became P.P. Kill and died 25 May 1865.
1845 — '46	Michael Fenlon. He died at Graigue at the age of 28 of typhus. He is buried at Myshall, where his epitaph gives the date of his death as 8 January 1947. Catholic Registry gives 9 January.
1847	Michael Maher.
1848	No second curate recorded.
1849 — '50	Thomas Maher. Possibly Fr. Thomas Maher, ordained 1847, P.P. Suncroft from November 1872 to his death 30 October 1883. Probably of the Ballyloughan or Donore family, while he had near friends, possibly brothers in South Green, Kildare.
1850 —	John Walsh, P.P. Clonbullogue 1856-63.

1853 — '54	Thomas Fenlon. Possibly T. Fenlon C.C. Kildare and Leighlin who died 20 April 1887. Ordained about 1851.
1855	John Dyer. Ordained about 1852. P.P. Leighlin 1870. P.P. Daingean 1881. Died 21 March 1885. Born in Ballykean, Geashill.
1852 — '58	Timothy O'Neill. Ordained about 1852, C.C. Killenure and died 13 February 1878.
1856	Andrew Hipwell. Also Marcus Bray and Tim O'Neill. Fr. Andrew Hipwell and C.C. Raheen and died March 1864.
1856 — '59	Marcus Bray. Died C.C. Graigue 11 January 1860. A relative of Bishop Nolan 1834-37. Vid Comerford I.122.
1859 — '60	Martin Nolan. P.P. Mountrath and P.P. Droicead Nua 1872. Died 14 June 1890.
1860 — '63	Augustine Kinsella. Ordained 1854, P.P. Caragh. Died 1 July 1905. A native of Cloneygowan. He was uncle of Fr. Austin Delaney P.P. Balyna who died 21 March 1951.
1861	No second curate.
1862	Patrick McCarthy. Possibly Dr. Daniel McCarthy P.P. Arles who died 20 July 1881. Vid Comerford I. 203.
1864 — '65	James O'Beirne. Either Fr. James O'Beirne B.A. Professor Carlow College 1838-42, who died in 1882, or his nephew and namesake who died P.P. Killeigh 4 June 1916. Both were natives of Monasterevan parish.
1864 — '66	Henry O'Neill, C.C. Arles, died 12 July 1876.
1866	No second curate.
1867 & 1869	Jerome Kelly. Ordained 1867, he was P.P. Rhode and died 26 August 1912. He was a native of Droicead Nua parish.
1867	T. Bourke.
1868	John Scully. A native probably of Mountmellick, he was ordained 1866.
1869	Simon McWey. Ordained 1869, he was P.P. Kilcock. He died 27 June 1898. A native of Slatty, Graiguebullen parish and was granduncle of Fr. Sean McWey C.C.
1870 — '74	James Lalor. Ordained 1870. He was P.P. Abbeyleix where he built the parish church. He was a first cousin of Bishop Foley and an uncle (or possibly granduncle) of Fr. E. Lalor present (1959) P.P. of Abbeyleix. Fr. James Lalor was a native of Irongrange, Baltinglass. He was a

	brother of Fr. Edward Lalor P.P. Allen 1889-1920.
1870 — '71	Fintan Phelan. Ordained 1856, P.P. Arles. Died March 1893.
1872	John Kelly. Possibly Fr. J. Kelly, ordained 1868, P.P. Ballyfin, died 26 January 1916. A native of Myshall.
1873 — '75	Laurence Hosey. Ordained 1867, was C.C. Ballyfin 1897-1903 and died in Portlaoise Hospital. A native of Ballinakill or Abbeyleix parish and a relative of Hosey's Primrose Hill, Carlow.
1875 — '81	Fr. Richard Byrne. Ordained 1873. He was C.C. Suncroft where he died 13 January 1900.
1876 — '81	Richard O'Brien. Ordained 1874. P.P. Myshall 1890 Paulstown 1901. Died 15 August 1934. A native of Newtown, Kelleigh. Uncle of Fr. James Dunne P.P. Hacketstown and Fr. James O'Brien P.P. Kill (1936-43).
1882	James Casey.
1882 — '87	J. Kirwan. Probably James Kirwan a native of Lower Grange. Ordained 1874, P.P. Kilcock. Died 15 February 1923. A brother Fr. Michael was C.C. Timahoe 1876-83.
1883	P. Clerke. Probably Patrick Clarke who was ordained 4 March 1852, C.C. Mountmellick and died 1861. Buried at Ballymacwilliam, Rhode parish of which he was a native. His epitaph in Latin is given in Comerford II. 324.
1884	Cristphor O'Brien. Fr. Christy O'Brien was a native of Edenberry. C.C. Rathoe. He died 31 August 1902.
1885 — '88	Peter H. Dunne, a native of Clonaslee, ordained 1873.
1888	T. Dowling. Fr. Thomas Dowling was P.P. Graignamanagh 1925-34.
1889	John Robinson, a native of Ballyna parish. Ordained 1887. Died 9 November 1920.
1890	Fr. McGee. Some of those who cannot easily be identified may be borrowed priests.
1891	T. Martin.
1891	John Kane, a native of Baltinglass parish, ordained 1891. P.P. Allen 1920, P.P. Kildare 1927. Died 13 October 1947.
1892	Peter Delaney. A native of Cush, Mountmellick, and an uncle of Fr. Austin Delaney P.P. Balyna. He died 20 November 1936.

1893   Christopher Coyne, a native of Carbury was ordained in 1893. P.P. Raheen 1920. Died 5 November 1954.

1894   Daniel O'Rourke, a native of Muinebeag parish, and brother of Fr. John P.P. Ballyfin. He was ordained 1887. P.P. St. Mullins 1907, Allen 1927. Died 28 January 1947.

1894 — '96   James Byrne. Probably Fr. James Byrne, a native of Graiguenaspidogue, Tinryland parish and brother of Fr. Thomas P.P. Stradbally 1927-34, and Fr. William P.P. Stradbally 1934-40. Fr. James was P.P. Carbury where he died 10 October 1919.

1895   John Robinson.

1896   M. McRedmond.

1897   Paul Dunphy. Ordained 1879. P.P. Rosenallis where he died 15 December 1940. He was uncle of Fr. James Dunphy P.P. Tinryland.

1897   Patrick Hipwell, a native of Oldtown, Mountrath, he was a brother of Fr. Michael P.P. Carbury. Fr. Pat became P.P. Ballyadams in 1923 and died 1 September 1934. He was ordained 1894.

1898   Edward Kinsella, a native of Leighlin parish and uncle of Fr. Edward Kinsella P.P. Daingean. He was Adm. Kill where he died 24 July 1911.

1900   John Gorman, a native of Killeen in Arles parish, he was ordained in 1891. He became P.P. Daingean in 1919. P.P. V.F. Mountmellick 1924. Died 28 July 1940.

1901   John James, a native of Carlow, he was ordained 1895 and was P.P. St. Mullins 1926, Rhode 1936. Died 21 December 1954.

1903   M. O'Brien. Fr. Mathew O'Brien a native of Clonbullogh and nephew of Fr. Lynam P.P. V.F. Muinebeag was ordained in 1903 and became P.P. Clonmore in 1932. He He died 14 May 1958.

1904 — '20   David Gorry, brother of Fr. Pat, P.P. Monasterevan. He was ordained in 1895 and became P.P. Tinryland 1925. Died 26 October 1933. A native of Cappyroe, Killeigh parish.

1904 — '05   William Rice, a brother of Fr. Michael P.P. Kilcock 1923-38, and a native of Sherwood, in Clonegal parish. He was ordained in 1899. P.P. Doonane 1921 and Carbury 1929, Kilcock 1938. He died 12 January 1952.

1906   John Foley, a native of Bananagole in Leighlin parish, a kinsman and a class fellow of Bishop Foley. He died 25 January 1917.

1907 — '15   James Dunne, a native of Ballingar, in Killeigh parish, he was ordained in 1901. He became P.P. Hacketstown 1930. Died 17 March 1956.

1918 — '21   Patrick Walsh. C.C. Clane, died 14 March 1925. Ordained 1907.

1921 — '26   Patrick Bennett, ordained 1911. P.P. Clonegal February 1945.

1922 — '28   Michael Hipwell, a native of Oldtown in Raheen parish. Ordained 1906. P.P. Doonane 1929, Carbury 1938 and died 11 December 1956.

1927 — '30   Andrew Farrell, a native of Leighlin parish. He was ordained in 1910, became P.P. Rathvilly in 1944. Died 23 March 1947.

1929 — '31   William Mahon, ordained 27 June 1926. P.P. Raheen November 1954.

1931 — '40   Jeremiah Maher, ordained 12 June 1927. P.P. Ballinakill September 1955.

1932 — '33   Joachim Doran, B.D. C.C. Tinryland, died 11 May 1937. Ordained 7 March 1925.

1934   William Grattan-Flood C.C. borrowed from Ferns.

1935 — '36   Joseph Griffin, ordained 16 June 1935.

1937   Maurice Murphy, ordained 10 June 1934. Died 26 November 1956, as C.C. Abbeyleix.

1938 — '40 (incl)   Michael Kelly, ordained 14 June 1908.

1941 — Mar '54   Jeremiah Bennett, ordained 13 June 1926. P.P. Caragh March 1954.

1941 — '45   Thomas Donohoe, ordained 11 June 1939.

1948 — '52   William Mathews, ordained 14 June 1931. P.P. Kill February 1957.

1951   John Mulcahy.

1952 — '54   John Boland. Ordained 22 June 1952.

1954 — '55   Jeremiah Murphy. Ordained 18 June 1939.

July 1955—Jan '61   John Walsh, ordained 19 June 1955.

1956 — Oct '58   Mathew Kelly, B.D. ordained 17 June 1956.

1958 — Aug '62   John Gahan, ordained 1955.

Jan 1961—Aug '68   Francis MacNamera ordained 19 June 1960.

Aug 1962—March '68   James Maher ordained 18 June 1961.

Bibliography

ANNALS AND CHRONICLES

Annals of Loch Cé (ed.) William Hennessey. Alexander Thom. 87/88, Abbey Street, Dublin.
Rother, D. *Analects de Rebus Catholicorum in Hibernia* (ed.). Patrick F. Moran, Bishop of Ossory, Dublin 1884.
Chartularies of St. Mary's Abbey Dublin, Gilbert, Longman. London 1884.
The Charters of the Cistercian Abbey of Duiske in the County of Kilkenny. Butler, C.M., Bernard, J.H. (ed.). *Proceedings of the Royal Irish Academy.* Vol. XXXV. Section c 1918-20.
Harl M.S. Charter 75, A5 printed by Clark: Cartae de Glamorgan No. 855. Birch Margam Abbey.
King's Collection M.S. compiled by Dr. Madden late 17th Century and revised by Harris N.L.I. and T.C.D. also as cited by Archdall, Monasticon Hibernicum.
Statuta Capitulorum Generalium Ordinis Cisterciensis ab annum 1116 *ad annum.* Canivez 1786 Louvain, 1933.
Stephen de Lexington (*Registrum Stephani de Lexington*) (ed.) B. Greisser. S. OCist, in Analicta S.O. Cist, 11, 1946.
T:C:D:MS 578 p. 1-4, 13-15 contains notes from the Charters in the Duiske register in the hand of Archbishop James Ussher, made when the original manuscript was in 'Mr. Chetham's Office' [died 1624]. There is also (p. 16-18) an Annals 1167-1570, mostly in Ussher's hand but titled by Bishop Anthony Dopping (died 1697) as *Annales Duiskenses.*

PRINTED AND CALENDARED MATERIAL

Berry and Morrisey. *Statute Rolls of Ireland.* 4 vols. Dublin for the Stationery Office. Brown & Nolan Ltd., 1939.
Bliss, W.H. Twemlow, J.A. Johnson, C (ed.) *Calendar of Papal Letters* (12 vols.) 1893-1933. London 1893.
Mills, J. *Calendar of the Justiciary Rolls Ireland* (1295-1303) Record Office Ireland, 1905.
Morrin, J. *Calendar of the Patent and Close Rolls of Chancery in Ireland* (Vol. II) Eliz. p. 285, 11, 15. Longman Green London 1862.
Morrin, J. *Calendar of the Patent and Close Rolls of Chancery in Ireland* London 1863. 16 Jas 1 p. 265, 338, 365.
Russel, C.W. and Prendergast, J.P. *Calendar of the State Papers relating to Ireland James I.* (1603-1606). Longman and Co, and Trubner and Co., London, 1872.

PUBLIC RECORDS OFFICE

Chartae, Privilegia et Immunitates. Transcripts of Charters and Privileges to Cities, Towns, Abbeys and other Bodies Corporate. 18 Henry 11 to 18 Richard 11 (1171-1395). The Irish Record Commission (1829-30). Hodges, Figgis, Dublin 1889.

PRINTED WORKS

Stanley muniments printed by W. de G. Birch, Collections towards the history of the Cistercian Abbey of Stanley in Wiltshire. *The Wiltshire Archaeological and Natural History Magazine,* 15 (1875), 239-279.
Braun, H. *English Abbeys,* London 1971.
Braunfels, W. *Monasteries of Western Europe,* London 1972.
Comerford Rev. M. *Collections of the Dioceses of Kildare and Leighlin.* Vol. III. Dublin 1886.
Conbhiú, C. *The Story of Mellifont,* Gill 1958. Dublin.
Curtis, E. *A History of Medieval Ireland 1086-1513.* Methuen & Co. London 1938.
Gale. *The Corporate System of Ireland.* London 1834.
Gwynn, A. Hadcock R.N. *Medieval Religious Houses in Ireland.* Longman, 1970.
Knowles, D.D. *The Religious Orders in England.* 3 vols. Cambridge 1951-59.
Leask, H.G. *Irish Churches and Monastic Buildings.* Dundalgan Press, Dundalk, 1960.
Lynch. *Legal Institution and Feudal Baronies in Ireland.* London. Longman, Rees, Orme, Brown & Green, 1830.
O'Leary, Patrick, William and John. *Graignamanagh Abbey,* Graignamanagh 1924.
Orpen, G.H. *Ireland Under the Normans.* 4 vols. (1911-20). Oxford: Clarendon Press.
Otway-Ruthven A.J. *A History of Medieval Ireland.* Ernest Benn Ltd. London, 1968.
Prendergast, J. *The Cromwellian Settlement of Ireland.* McGlashan and Gill, Dublin 1875.
Phillips, W.H. *History of the Church of Ireland from the earliest times to the present day.* Vol. I, II, III. Humphrey, Milford, London, 1933.
Ralegh Radford C.A. *Strata Florida Abbey.* Ancient Monuments and Historic Buildings. Ministry of Works H.M.S.O.
Simington. *Book Survey and Distribution.* Co. Kilkenny. Public

Record Office, Dublin.

Sweetman. *Calendar of Documents relating to Ireland.* 1302-07. Vol. 5 (pp. 264-323). London. Longman & Co. and Trubner & Co., 1886.

Fiants of Elizabeth Nos. 290, 175.

Ware, James. *The Antiquities and History of Ireland.* Vol. I and II (ed.) Walter Harris. Longman, Green and Co. London, 1705, also Dublin, 1764.

Watt, J.A. *The Church and the Two Nations in Medieval Ireland.* Cambridge Studies in Medieval Life and Thought. Third Series. Vol. 3. Cambridge University Press, 1970.

White, N.B. *Irish Monastic and Episcopal Deeds.* Dublin Stationery Office, 1936. pp. 193-8.

White, N.B. *Extents of Irish Monastic Possessions 1540-41.* The Stationery Office, Dublin, 1943.

Archdall, M. *Monasticon Hibernicum 354.* Includes Inquisition 9 Elizabeth from Auditor Generals' Office — Luke White. Dublin. 1886.

References

CHAPTER 1: *The Celtic Twilight*
1. Bowen E.G., Saints, Seaways and Settlements in the Celtic Lands, 1969, p. 128.
2. Gwynn A. Hadcock R.N. *Medieval Religious Houses 1970.* p. 136.
3. *Ibid.* p. 132.
4. *Ibid.* p. 130.
5. *Ibid.* p. 134.
6. *Ibid.* p. 142.
7. *Ibid.* p. 132.
8. *Ibid.* p. 137.
9. *Ibid.* p. 129.
10. *Ibid.* p. 145. Kinalehin Galway. Diocese Clonfert c. 1252.

CHAPTER 2: *The Arrival of the Cistercians*
1. Gwynn A. Hadcock R.N. *Medieval Religious Houses 1970.* p. 28-46.
2. Bernard 21. Letter no. 383.

CHAPTER 3: *The Abbey's Charter*
1. Gwynn A. Hadcock R.N. *Medieval Religious Houses 1970.* p. 136.
2. *Ibid.* p. 136.
3. *Ibid.* p. 136.
4. *Ibid.* p. 136.
5. *Ibid.* p. 136.
6. Comerford M. *Collections Relating to the Dioceses of Kildare and Leighlin.* Third Series-Diocese of Leighlin 1886. p. 200. Note. The witnesses to this Charter include St. Laurence O'Toole who became Archbishop of Dublin in 1162 and King Dermod Mac Murrough who died in 1177. This puts the date of the Charter between 1162-1177.
7. Butler and Bernard. *Proceedings of the Royal Irish Academy.* The Charters of the Cistercian Abbey of Duiske in the County of Kilkenny. Vol. XXXV. 1918-20 Dublin. p. 21.
8. Butler and Bernard, *op. cit.* p. 21.
9. Colmcille. Rev. Fr. O.C.S.O. *The Story of Mellifont,* Dublin, 1958. p. 4 citing Canivez 119:43.
10. *Ibid.* p. 48 citing Canivez 1201:40.
11. *Ibid.* p. 48 citing Canivez 1202:32.
12. *Ibid.* p. 48 citing Canivez 1202:33.

Note (1)
Fr. Colmcille in *The Story of Mellifont* (p. 49) states that 'The name Stoquella has been something of a puzzle to scholars and students of Cistercian history. Dr. Joseph Canivez in his edition of the Statuta suggests Byland near Stocking, while other writers seem to be content to write it off as unidentified if not unidentifiable. However, taking it for granted that there is here question of the foundation of Duiske, by William Marshall the identification which naturally suggests itself, is Stanley in Wiltshire, later the Mother house of the Abbey of Duiske.

The Abbey of Duiske was founded from Stanley in 1204 and the founder was William Marshall. A statute of the General Chapter of that year referring apparently to the monastery of Escharlis in France domus Scarleiae should we think be interpreted as referring rather to the house of Stanley in Wiltshire England.

13. Comerford M. *Collections Relating to the Dioceses of Kildare and Leighlin.* Third Series-Diocese of Leighlin 1886. Charter granted by William Earl of Pembroke. p. 201.
14. Butler and Bernard. *Proceedings of the Royal Irish Academy.* The Charters of the Cistercian Abbey of Duiske in the County of Kilkenny Vol. XXXV. 1918-20. Dublin p. 25.
15. Comerford Rev. M. *Collections relating to the dioceses of Kildare and Leighlin.* Vol. III p. 203.
16. T.C.D.M.S.E.3.15 fol. 11,6.
17. Butler and Bernard. *Proceedings of the Royal Irish Academy.* The Charters of the Cistercian Abbey of Duiske in the County of Kilkenny. Vol. XXXV. 1918-20. Dublin p. 13. Conuentus de Starleya uenit in Hiberniam, qui primo habitauit apud Lochmeran iuxta Kilkenniam, deinde apud Athnamolt, postea apud Castrum, ultimo in loco ubi nunc sunt, dicto Duisque alias Sancti Saluatoris.'
18. *Ibid.* above passage p. 13 so. o.

CHAPTER 4: *Splendid Restraint*
1. Braunfels, W. 1972. p. 45-46.
2. Braun, H. 1971. p. 70.

3. *Ibid.* p. 72. In medieval days it was customary to stop six-teen men as they entered the church porch and make each place his foot behind that of his neighbour in order to assess the local pole.
4. Colmcille, Fr. *The Story of Mellifont*, Dublin. 1958 p. 9.
5. Braunfels, W. *Op. cit.* p. 85.
6. T.C.D.M.SE3.15 fol 11,6.
7. T.C.D.M.SE3.15 fol 11,6.
8. Butler and Bernard, *Proceedings of the Royal Irish Academy*. The Charters of the Cistercian Abbey of Duiske in the County of Kilkenny Vol. XXXV. 1918-20. Dublin, p. 170.

CHAPTER 5: *Building the Abbey*
1. Lacock Cartulary, f. 30b.
2. Waterman, D.M. *Ulster Journal of Archaeology*. Vol. 38, 1970. p. 63-75.
3. *Ibid.* p. 65.
4. *Ibid.* p. 63.
5. *Ibid.* p. 68.
6. Comerford R.M. *Collections relating to the Dioceses of Kildare and Leighlin*. Dublin. 1886. p. 215.
7. *Ibid.* p. 215. Note 'Mr. Cheevers' appears in a Deed (1812) as a trustee of Duiske Abbey.
8. Butler and Bernard. *Proceedings of the Royal Irish Academy*. The Charters of the Cistercian Abbey of Duiske in the County of Kilkenny. Vol. XXXV. Dublin. p. 15, also Comerford. p. 204.
9. *Ibid.* p. 26.
10. *Ibid.* p. 49.
11. *Ibid.* p. 58, also Comerford. p. 204.
12. *Ibid.* p. 64, also Comerford. p. 204.

CHAPTER 6: *The Monastic Estate*
1. Butler and Bernard. *Proceedings of the Royal Irish Academy*. The Charters of the Cistercian Abbey of Duiske in the County of Kilkenny. Vol. XXXV. Dublin. pp. 17-21.
2. *Ibid.* p. 26.
3. *Ibid.* p. 39.
4. *Ibid.* p. 35, p. 67.

CHAPTER 7: *The Old Abbey*
1. Gwynn A. Hadcock R.N. *Medieval Religious Houses*. 1970. p. 138.
2. Butler and Bernard. *Proceedings of the Royal Irish Academy*. The Charters of the Cistercian Abbey of Duiske in the County of Kilkenny. Vol. XXXV. Dublin. p. 10.
3. *Ibid.* p. 11.
4. *Ibid.* p. 43.
5. *Ibid.* p. 43.
6. *Ibid.* p. 45.
7. *Ibid.* p. 83.
8. *Ibid.* p. 93.

9. *Ibid.* p. 100.
10. *Ibid.* p. 101.
11. *Ibid.* p. 114.
12. *Ibid.* p. 117.
13. *Ibid.* p. 118-119.
14. *Ibid.* p. 121.
15. *Ibid.* p. 137.
16. *Ibid.* p. 140.

Note
Table, p. 50: Sources:- The foundation charter has been printed by Butler and Bernard in 'The Charters of the Abbey of Duiske' (*PRIA* XXXV, 1918) and the extent made at the dissolution of the monastic property is also reproduced in the same work.
I.M.E. 193-8.
MH354 (includes inq.9. Elizabeth from Auditor General's Office).
Calendar of Documents V, 264, 323.
Fiants: Elizabeth nos 290, 1175.
CPR: 36 Elizabeth (Morrin ii, 285) 11, 15 and 16 Jas 1 (pp. 265, 338, 365).
BSD Co. Kilkenny and OS and DS Maps.

CHAPTER 8: *Quality of Land*
1. Dr. Conroy. *An Foras Taluntais*. Carlow in conversation.
2. Knowles D.D. *The Monastic Orders in England* 1948. p. 70-71.
3. Bernard, J.H., Butler, M.C. Ed. 1918-1920. p. 124-5.
4. *Ibid.* p. 125.
5. *Ibid.* p. 126.
6. White. N.B. *Extents of Irish Monastic Possessions*. Dublin Stationery Office. 1943. p. 194.
7. *Ibid.* p. 195.
8. *Ibid.* p. 195.
9. *Ibid.* p. 195.
10. Bernard, J.H. Butler M.C. Ed. 1918-1920. p. 140'
11. White N.B. *Extents of Irish Monastic Possessions*. p. 194.
12. *Ibid.* p. 195.
13. *Ibid.* p. 195.
14. Bernard, J.H. Butler M.C. Ed. 1918-1920. p. 110.
15. *Ibid.* p. 68.

CHAPTER 9 [1]: *The Abbey and the Community*
1. White N.B. *Extents of Irish Monastic Possessions*. Dublin 1943 Formula p. 194.
2. *Ibid.* p. 194.
3. *Ibid.* p. 194.
4. *Ibid.* p. 194.
5. *Ibid.* p. 194.
6. *Ibid.* p. 194.
7. *Ibid.* p. 195.
8. *Ibid.* p. 195.

9. *Ibid*. p. 196.
10. *Ibid*. p. 2.
11. *Ibid*. p. 8.
12. *Ibid*. p. 354.
13. *Ibid*. p. 44.
14. *Ibid*. p. 196.
15. *Ibid*. p. 196.
16. *Ibid*. p. 196.
17. *Ibid*. p. 196.
18. *Ibid*. p. 194.
19. *Ibid*. p. 196.
20. *Ibid*. p. 196.
21. *Ibid*. p. 214.
22. *Ibid*. p. 269.
23. *Ibid*. p. 18.
24. *Ibid*. p. 196.

CHAPTER 9 [2]: *The Abbey Treasury*
1. Birch, W. de G. 'Collections towards the history of the Cistercian Abbey of Stanley in Wiltshire.' *The Wiltshire Archaeological and Natural History Magazine*, 15 (1875).

CHAPTER 10: *Times of Change*
1. Comerford, M. Collections relating to the Diocese of Kildare and Leighlin. 1886. p. 227.

CHAPTER 11: *The Monk's Code*
1. Watt, J.A. *The Church and the Two Nations in Medieval Ireland*. Cambridge Univ. Press, 1970. p. 87.
2. *Ibid*. citing Canivez (1202.26).
3. *Ibid*. p. 89.
4. *Ibid*. p. 89 citing. *The Charters of the Cistercian Abbey of Duiske in the County of Kilkenny*. Ed. C.M. Butler and J.H. Bernard PRIA 35 (1918) sect C 19,44.
5. Watt. *Ibid*. p. 90 citing Canivez. Statuta 2 (1227.29).
6. *Ibid*. p. 90)
7. *Ibid*. p. 90)   Canivez Statuta 2 (1227.36)
8. *Ibid*. p. 90)
9. This has been shown in Chapter 7. Butler and Bernard.
10. *Ibid*. p. 91, and Butler and Bernard. pp. 13-14. Canivez Statuta 1 (1201.40), 1202.32, 1204.22. Colmcille *The Story of Mellifont* p. 48-9. Watt, J.A. *The Church and The Two Nations in Medieval Ireland*. 1970.
11. *Ibid*. p. 91.
12. *Ibid*. p. 91.
13. *Ibid*. p. 93.
14. *Ibid*. p. 95.
15. *Ibid*. p. 95.
16. *Ibid*. p. 95.
17. *Ibid*. p. 96.
18. *Ibid*. p. 96.
19. *Ibid*. p. 96.

20. *Ibid*. p. 96.
21. *Ibid*. p. 97.
22. *Ibid*. p. 98.
23. *Ibid*. p. 99.
24. *Ibid*. p. 101-103.
25. Bernard, J.H., Butler, M.C. Ed. 1918-19. p. 79.
26. *Ibid*. p. 81.
27. Mills. *Calendar of Justiciary Rolls*. Vol. III. (1914). p. 174.
28. *Ibid*. Vol. I. (1905). p. 21.
29. Bernard, J.H. Butler M.C. *op. cit*. p. 66.
30. Gwynn, A. Hadcock, R.N. *Medieval Religious Houses Ireland* p. 140.
31. *Ibid*. p. 136.

CHAPTER 11 [2]: *Graignamanagh and the Papacy*
1. Bernard, J.H., Butler, M.C. Ed. 1918-19. p. 58.

CHAPTER 12: *The Abbey and the Town*
1. Watt J.A. *The Church and Two Nations in Medieval Ireland* (1970). p. 106.
2. *Ibid*. p. 106.
3. *Ibid*. p. 106.
4. *Ibid*. p. 106.
5. *Ibid*. p. 107.
6. Bliss, Twemlow, Johnston. Calendar of Papal Register 1240. Dec. 14. Greg IX *Regesta* Vol. XX p. 192.
7. *Ibid*. 11 Boniface IX. p. 295.
8. *Ibid*. *Lateran Regesta* Vol. CCCCX. p. 434-35.
9. *Ibid*. C.P.L. 1447.

CHAPTER 13: *The Knight of Duiske Abbey*
1. White N.B. *Extents of Irish Monastic Possessions* 1541.
2. O'Leary, Patrick and William and John. *Graignamanagh Abbey* 1924. p. 21.
3. Bernard, J.H. Butler, M.C. Ed. 1918-20. p. 106.
4. *Ibid*. p. 105, 106.
5. *Ibid*. p. 105, 106.
5. *Ibid*. p. 91.
6. *Ibid*. p. 91, 92.
7. *Ibid*. p. 89.
8. *Ibid*. p. 107.
9. *Ibid*. p. 107.
10. *Ibid*. p. 105, 106.
11. *Ibid*. p. 89.
12. *Ibid*. p. 14, 15, 22.
13. *Ibid*. p. 16, 17.
14. *Ibid*. p. 88.
15. *Ibid*. p. 89, 91.
16. *Ibid*. p. 91, 92.
17. *Ibid*. p. 91, 92.
18. *Ibid*. p. 89.
19. *Ibid*. p. 91, 92, 106, 107.

20. Ch. Rem. Roll Du 66 Ed. 11.
21. Charter Roll T.L. 17 John and Chartae Privilegia & Immunitates Irish Record Commission, 1829-30. p. 37.
22. 34, 35, 36 Eliza. Ch. Rem. Roll Dublin.
23. Chartae Privilegia "Immunitates, Irish Record Commission 1829-30. p. 47.
24. Butler, J.H. Butler C.M. Ed. 1918-19. p 107.
25. *Ibid.* p. 91.
26. *Ibid.* p. 106.
27. Mills, J. Calendar of Justiciary Rolls Edward I. Vol. I 1295-1303 Vol. II 1305-1307 Vol. III 1308-14 (1914). p. 466.

CHAPTER 14: *Caring for the People*
1. Bernard, J.H. Butler, M.C. Ed. 1918-19. p. 37.
2. *Ibid.* p. 12.
3. *Ibid.* p. 21.
4. *Ibid.* p. 42.
5. *Ibid.* p. 88.
6. *Ibid.* p. 106.
7. Mills, J. Calendar of Justiciary Rolls published 1914. Vol. II (1305-1307) pp. 466.
8. *Ibid.* p. 126. Vol. II.
9. Bernard, J.H. Butler, M.C.Ed. 1918-19. p. 188 no 2.

CHAPTER 15: *The Harp that Once*
1. T.C.D. MSE3.15 fol 11,6.
2. Otway — Ruthven, A.J., 1968. p. 268. Otway — Ruthven's ref. 52 (Genealogical Office, MS. 192 93-94).

CHAPTER 16: *The Dissolution*
1. Bernard, J.H. Butler M.C. Ed. 1918-19. p. 101, 102.
2. *Ibid.* p. 102.
3. E.W. Hughes in conversation.
4. Hardiman's *Minstrelsy.* p. 357 (notes).
5. *Ibid.* p. 357.
6. *Ibid.* p. 357.
7. *Ibid.* p. 357.

CHAPTER 17: *A Town Remembers*
1. Colmcille, Rev. Fr. *The Story of Mellifont*, Dublin 1958, p. 156.
2. Butler, J.H. Bernard, M.C. Ed. 1918-19. p. 132.
3. *Ibid.* p. 143. citing. Calendar Papal Letters. Vol. X. p. 497.
4. Butler, J.H. Bernard, M.C. Ed. 1918-19. p. 149.
5. Roman, R.V. *The Reformation in Dublin* 1536-1558. p. 176. They had granted in the matter of money, the subsidy, the twentieth of their revenues and the first fruits of their Abbey in the event of a new Abbot.
6. Morrin, J. *Calendar of Patent and Close Rolls Chancery*, Ireland, Vol. 1, p. 55.
7. Butler, J.H. Bernard, *op. cit.* p. 16-17.

8. *Ibid.* p. 155.
9. White N.B. Extents of Irish Monastic Possessions. p. 197.
10. Bernard, J:H: Butler, *op. cit.* p. 161.
11. *Ibid.* p. 162
12. *Ibid.* p. 162
13. *Ibid.* p. 164 Calendar State Papers, 31 July 1566.
14. *Ibid.* p. 164
15. *Ibid.* p. 164 Fiants Elizabeth No. 6441, 22 September 1600
16. *Ibid.* p. 164
17. *Ibid.* p. 167
18. *Ibid.* p. 167

CHAPTER 18: *Epilogue*
1. Deed 1812 by courtesy of E.W. Hughes
2. *Ibid.*
3. *Ibid.*
4. *Ibid.*
5. White N.B. *Extents of Irish Monastic Possessions.* p. 198.

Index

O'Connor, Crobhdearg, 27
O'Daly, Carol, 86-88
O'Daly, Donogh Mor, 86-88
O'Devany, Cornelius, 105
O'Hurley, Dermot, 105
O'Kavanagh, Charles, 91-93
O'Leary, Edward, 104
O'Leary, James, 104
O'Leary, John, 100
O'Leary, Patrick, 100, 102-106
O'Ryan, Dermot, 17, 45
O'Ryan, Henry Fitz Henry, 48
Odrufyn, Thomas, 73
Odrufyn, Nicholas, 74
Ohekyr, Conechor, 78
Old Abbey *see* Shanavanister
Old Grange, 42, 72, 75
Olto, Cardinal of St. Nicholas in Carure, 73
Orpen, T, 42, 44
Ossory, Abbey of, 17
Ossory, Diocese of, 11
Owens, Parson, 97

Paladius, 11
Pannyth, Bendinus, 47
Patrick, Saint, 11
Phillip, Abbot of Duiske, 54, 74
Phillip, Abbot of Jerpoint, 18, 19, 48, 62, 73
Plytevin, Henry le, 64
Poer, John le, 81, 82, 83
Porter, William, 90
Portgrenan, 55
Poultmuntath, 55
Powerstown, 45
Prendergast, Elias de, 81, 82
Prendergast, Philip de, 18, 19, 81

Quency, Matilda de, 82

Raheendonore, 57
Rathboghall, 41
Roche, Lord Milo, 86
Roche, Gilbert de la, 86
Roche, Henry Fitz Henry, 55
Roche, Fr. Mathew, 97
Roche, Philip de la, 87-88
Roche, Raymond, 86
Roche, Tom, 104
Roheendus, 41
Rokby, Thomas, 19
Roscrea, 16

Rossdama, 41
Rossiter, Ignatius, 98
Rous, Hugh le, 33, 34
Rous, Peter le, 78
Roth, Henry, 90
Ryan, William, 93

St. Florence, Richard de, 78
St. Florence, William de, 78
St. John, 34
Saint Mary's Abbey, 13, 58, 92
St. Maur, Nicholas de, 64
Saint Moling, 13
Salernum, John of, 45
Serman, Robert, 47
Shanavanister, Grange of, 45, 54
Shorthall, Gilbert, 19
Sisters of Mercy, 97
Slieve Ardagh, 39
Smith, Hugh, 93
Smyth, John, 73
Stanley, Abbey of, 32, 59
Stanley, Abbot of, 18, 19, 32, 61
Stoquela, Abbot of *see* Stanley, Abbot of
Strata Florida, Abbey of, 26
Strongbow, 18

Tabernar, Henry, 78
Tannur, Andrew, 78
Teste, Leonard, 47
Thomas, Abbot of Graignamanagh, 52, 73
Thomas, Abbot of Jerpoint, 47
Tikerlevan, 41, 57, 64, 66
Tinnahinch, 60
Tinnahinch Castle, 94
Tintern Abbey, 29, Suppressed, 92
Trahern, Edmund, 90
Trully, David, 88
Tudor, Mary, 92
Tullachany, 34, 39, 41, 54, 57, 58, 64, 66, 94
Turneronde, John, 82
Twelve Apostles of Ireland, 11

Urban VI, Pope, 73

Valle, Walter de, 19
Walerand, Robert, 64
Walsh, Billy, 102
Walsh, Philip, 84

Watt, J. A., 62
Welbore, Henry, 98
Wengum, Gilbert, 83
White, Thomas, 54
Whithay, Richard, 82
William, Bishop of Bath, 64
Wood Grange, 58, 64